TRAGEDY IS NOT ENOUGH

Tragedy Is Not Enough

by

KARL JASPERS

translated by

HARALD A. T. REICHE, HARRY T. MOORE, AND
KARL W. DEUTSCH

ARCHON BOOKS
1969

The Bibliography, Notes, and Index were prepared by
Harald A. T. Reiche

SBN: 208 00730 X
Library of Congress Catalog Card Number: 69-13628
Printed in the United States of America

Contents

Tragedy and Karl Jaspers

The ideas in the pages translated here took shape amid the ruins of Germany during and after the Second World War. Their author, Karl Jaspers, lived in Germany during the years when so many Germans followed Hitler in an enterprise of conquest that ended in destruction and defeat. Throughout the years of war, this quiet professor of philosophy had to listen not merely for the sound of airplanes and the rush of bombs, but for the more terrible sounds of life under dictatorship: the tramp of boots in the corridor, the knock at the door, the official voice that might announce arrest for him or for those dear to him.

During those years, Jaspers lived with the threat of tragedy in his own home, physically and spiritually. For Karl Jaspers, though a figure in world philosophy, is a German thinker, and his roots are deep in the German tradition. His own work is living proof of the continued existence of a deeper Germany, a Germany of thinkers and poets. It is in the great German tradition, which combines vast learning with rich imagination, and an insistence on honesty, consistency, and character with a startling ability to gain unexpected insights from paradoxes and contradictions, and from those "jagged breaks" in the

smooth surface of reality where so much of the underlying
structure is revealed.

Despite all tyranny, error, and misfortune, this deep,
humane tradition has never died in Germany. The foreign
prisoners of the Nazis knew it well in 1945 in the concen-
tration camp of Buchenwald, when, at the celebration of
their liberation, they invited their former German fellow-
prisoners to take an equal place with the liberated prisoners
from all other countries, side by side with all the other
heroes and victims of the common struggle for human
dignity and freedom.

Despite everything the Nazis did — and everything the
passivity, gullibility, and subservience of millions of other
Germans let them do — the generation of quiet and open
resistance to callousness and evil, the generation of Ernst
Wiechert and Thomas Mann, of Albert Schweitzer and
Karl Jaspers, and of the thousands of martyrs in the con-
centration camps, can stand comparison with any previous
generation that made its contribution to the intellectual
and moral heritage of German civilization.

Just because of his inalienable place in that German
tradition, Karl Jaspers must have suffered deeply in seeing
his people succumb to the nightmare of Nazi rule. Over
and above the pressure of the terror, he must have felt
for years the subtle and insidious pull of Nazi propaganda,
calling upon him not to stand aside from a popular movement that pretended to speak in the name of all Germany.

Yet Jaspers did not bend and did not break. Refugees
from Germany have told how he remained true to his con-

victions throughout the years of terror. After the war, he was one of the first of the very few German thinkers who had lived in Germany throughout the war to dare to face the question of the moral guilt and responsibility of the German people for the coming of that war and the atrocities committed in its course.

In his book, *Die Schuldfrage — The Question of Guilt* — he told his countrymen that they could not escape their responsibility for the deeds of a Nazi government which most of them had not resisted, and which many of them had supported in many ways. However true it might be, he said, that other nations, governments, and individuals could not escape their share of responsibility for the catastrophe that had occurred, no pointing to the guilt of others could free the German people from the burden of the guilt that was their own — a guilt that required nothing less than complete honesty and long, difficult, and thorough inner reorientation.

This was hardly popular writing in a post-war Germany whose people seemed to have little left except hunger and resentment, pride and self-pity, amidst the ruins of their homes. Yet it was perhaps something that had to be written by a philosopher who had devoted so much of his thought and of his life to the values of compassion and the will to truth.

Perhaps he had to pay a price for his candor. After the publication of his book on *The Question of Guilt,* attacks on Jaspers increased in the German world of letters. Whether by coincidence or not, the man who held out

in Germany during the worst years of war and Nazi
rule is teaching now at the University of Basel, in
Switzerland. Whether and when a great German university will succeed in bringing Karl Jaspers back to
Germany again may be a test of some sort for the waning
of the Nazi heritage and the growth of a democratic climate
of opinion in that country.

Jaspers himself has been more concerned with insight
and compassion than with resentment. A psychologist as
much as a philosopher, he has sought to understand, even
though he has not been afraid to give judgment. There
has been much in the tragedy of Germany, and of German
youth since 1933, that has called for understanding and
compassion: the promises believed, the hopes betrayed,
the heroism, the suffering, and the endurance of thousands
and millions — all that was destined to end in ruin, disillusionment, and failure.

It is for this disillusioned generation, this generation
of defeat, that Jaspers is writing about tragedy. But
writing out of the depth of a tragic experience that is
both theirs and his, writing as the witness of the shattering
of a vast enterprise of a great country, Jaspers has written
about tragedy — about the reality and significance of tragedy — for all men everywhere.

Writing with this knowledge of tragedy, Jaspers draws
a sharp distinction between tragic reality and tragic pose —
a distinction that becomes a devastating criticism of Nazi
ideology and its present-day offshoots.

He unmasks the blindness of "the average so-called man of determination," who became a German idol in the age of Hitler and Goering, and who may again become an idol in many countries in the world-wide race for atom bombs — the man who rushes into action because he can no longer bear the burden of continuing responsibility. "Those who have nothing but determination," Jaspers reminds us, "in their forceful assurance, their unthinking obedience, their unquestioning brutality — they are in reality caught up in the narrowness of their illusions." Theirs is "a dull-witted enthusiasm for that drastic and immediate resort to action which characterizes men passively subservient to their impulses."

Jaspers sees through the pose that treats tragedy as the proper attribute of chosen heroes, a chosen race, or a chosen set of dignified problems. In this aesthetic and dramatic attitude, so reminiscent of Wagner's *Götterdämmerung* and of Hitler's posturing during the fall of Berlin,

> . . . tragedy becomes the privilege of the exalted few — all others must be content to be wiped out indifferently in disaster. Tragedy then becomes a characteristic not of man, but of a human aristocracy. As the code of privilege, this philosophy gives us comfort by pandering to our self-esteem. . . . Misery — hopeless, meaningless, heart-rending, destitute and helpless misery — cries out for help. But the reality of all this misery without greatness is pushed aside as unworthy of notice by minds that are blind with exaltation.

Jaspers' summary of the perversions of tragic knowledge into varieties of would-be tragic philosophy becomes an

indictment not merely of the Nazi regime, but of all
varieties of totalitarian pessimism:

> Wherever total lack of faith seeks to parade as form, it
> finds the philosophy of nothing-but-tragedy well suited as
> a camouflage for nothingness. Tragic grandeur is the prop
> whereby the arrogant nihilist can elevate himself to the pathos
> of feeling himself a hero. Where seriousness has been lost,
> an experience of pseudo-seriousness is produced by the violent
> stimulant of tragedy. . . . Such perversion of tragic philosophy
> then sets free the turmoil of dark impulses: the delight in
> meaningless activity, in torturing and in being tortured, in de-
> struction for its own sake, in the raging hatred against the
> world and man, coupled with the raging hatred against one's
> own despised existence.

At the opposite pole from such fraudulent grandeur,
Jaspers unmasks the hollowness of another attitude to
tragedy, the attitude of apathy or complete withdrawal,
where tragic knowledge has shrunk "to a mere pinpoint of
self-assertion."

Such warnings against perversions of tragic knowledge
seem relevant indeed in a book published in post-war
Germany where millions know tragedy as real. But is this
book then not merely a philosopher's and psychiatrist's
prescription for the special case of Germany? Why should
we care about tragedy here, in a country as well equipped
and traditionally optimistic as the United States?

One answer to this question seems obvious. Within our
lifetime, our own cities may become victims of war. Never
since the year 1813, when a British landing party burned
the city of Washington, D.C., have we been so thoroughly

within the range of the weapons of other nations. Never before have so many of us lived huddled together so closely on so few exposed bombing targets. It may take great effort and great good fortune, as well as what some of us might call the grace of God, if our own experiences are not to make us yet a suitable public for philosophies of tragedy.

Another answer might point to the vogue of existentialism and neo-orthodoxy as contemporary styles of thought, and to the widespread current emphasis on the weakness and incapacity of man. After a century of optimism, today's generation again wonders how much truth there may be in the mood of tragic awareness indicated succinctly by Jaspers: "Man's mind fails and breaks down in the very wealth of its potentialities. Every one of these potentialities, as it becomes fulfilled, provokes and reaps disaster."

There is still another answer, and it may be the most significant of all. Jaspers is the philosopher of openness, of readiness, of restless movement, of humility, and of compassion. "The hovering philosopher," he has been called, and there is much in his writing to suggest that he might accept the appellation. His is the great refusal of the idolatry of excessive commitment and of the premature closure of the search. This style of philosophic thought, and the insights Jaspers has achieved with it, may well be relevant and suggestive in our own search for understanding ourselves and our own situation.

What, then, does Karl Jaspers believe in? It is impossible to give in this space an outline of the philosophy of a lifetime, or even of the as-yet-untranslated thousand-page work *On Truth — Von der Wahrheit* — of which the present book forms a section. All we can do here is to try to gain an impression of three concepts that are crucial in Jaspers' thinking: the Encompassing; man's experience of limits and transcendence; and the will to communication. The impressions of these concepts will be based not only on the present book, but also on other works by Karl Jaspers, including *Von der Wahrheit*. They will be, furthermore, the impressions of a writer whose own interests have largely been concerned with political and social science, and in philosophic matters primarily with the operational philosophy of science and the theory of communication. It is quite possible that the same basic ideas of Jaspers might evoke a different echo in the minds of readers with a different background or concern. If the brief sketch that follows here will induce readers, therefore, to go on for themselves to a more extended study of the original works of Karl Jaspers, it will have served its purpose.

Imagine yourself climbing a mountain and looking out across the land. You see a large collection of well-defined objects, bounded by the horizon. You do not see what is beyond the horizon, but you have reason to think that that which is beyond the horizon and which, unseen, is surrounding or encompassing your present field of vision, is quite as real as the things you look upon.

As you climb higher, your horizon recedes. Some things which earlier had been part of the unseen and undefined Encompassing are now well-defined objects in the landscape you can see. But no matter how high you climb or fly, there will always be an encompassing reality beyond your horizon and beyond the boundaries of your area of knowledge and cognition. You may expect to push back these boundaries time after time, but you cannot seriously hope to abolish or exhaust the vaster reality behind them — the inescapable reality that encompasses all we know and all we think.

This encompassing reality can neither be known nor charted. To the extent that parts of it become known, they cease to be parts of the Encompassing and become parts of our field of knowledge and action. This field of knowledge and action, however, is always small compared to the vastness of the Encompassing which is in some aspects another name for the universe as a whole; and the knowledge and the operations of verification of which we dispose are inevitably non-exhaustive, relatively superficial, and potentially misleading as regards the hidden or deeper aspects even of the things that seem familiar.

Of course, the horizon seen from a lookout point is not the only limit to our field of vision. There is the equivalent of a horizon at the limit of accuracy of every scientific instrument or operation; at the surface of every object we look at; at the boundaries of the very large and the very small, the metagalaxy as well as the electron; and there is a boundary within each one of us at the limits of our self-awareness of which we only know that it does not exhaust the total content of our personality.

Beyond each of these shifting but ever-present limits is uncharted, encompassing reality. If the totality of our outer and inner knowledge furnishes the background for our knowledge for each particular thing, then the uncharted and inexhaustible Encompassing surrounds all our horizons and can be thought of as the background of all backgrounds.

We can neither know the structure of this Encompassing, nor verify any proposition about it as a whole. All we can accurately know or verify are propositions concerning particular small parts of the Encompassing, which are in the process of becoming detached from it and becoming incorporated in our particular field of knowledge and action.

Yet, though we cannot know the Encompassing as a whole, we cannot live without making assumptions about it, explicit or implied. All such assumptions are surmises, whether derived from the extrapolation of particular scientific measurements, from intuition, or from prophetic inspiration. Even so, our surmises are not merely arbitrary. They can be better or worse, sensitive or obtuse, fantastic or in tune with at least some patterns of reality. At the limits of our knowledge, we must needs try to transcend them, and we can be guided in this effort by the general information offered or suggested to us by specific objects. Every stone, every event not merely exists in itself, but can also function as a symbol, a code, or — in Jaspers' term — as a *chiffre* or cipher, corresponding loosely or accurately to some pattern in the encompassing reality.

Though our surmises concerning the Encompassing are fallible, and though we may "fear and tremble" that we may have misread the cipher and misunderstood the message, we needs must live by faith — that is, by the depth and effectiveness of our commitment to these surmises and to our unending search for better ones.

As these remarks suggest, Jaspers' idea of the Encompassing implies the ideas of limits and of transcendence. Man always and inevitably encounters limits to his knowledge and his power. There is a final limit for each man and for each finite structure, but no limit is absolute. Each can be overcome, but sometimes only at the price of destroying the personality or structure that set out to overcome it.

Tragedy, therefore, is fundamental and inevitable in human life. Tragedy occurs wherever awareness exceeds power; and particularly where awareness of a major need exceeds the power to satisfy it. The thirst that cannot as yet be quenched, the compassion with human suffering that cannot as yet be alleviated — these are inseparable from human existence. As human powers grow, and old needs are satisfied, awareness will have grown as much or more, and new needs and new tragedies will have been discovered. Tragedy thus may be said to occur at the margin of awareness beyond power, where men can sense and suffer beyond their ability to act and win success — a margin that can and should shift its position, but which perhaps does not shrink.

The alternative to recurrent tragedy, the abolition of this margin of awareness, might well destroy the humanity of man. A person whose limits of awareness should coincide precisely with his limits of successful action would be unlikely to suffer.

And a person or a government whose power to act substantially exceeded its limits of awareness would be as blind as a racing automobile at night without headlights. It would soon become an engine of destruction and eventually wreck itself. The price we pay to avoid such blindness or stagnation consists in the perennial possibility of tragedy, in the potential heartbreak which remains implicit in the fact that our eyes can see farther than our hands can reach.

Man's awareness not merely must exceed his power; it may also exceed the limits of his self-preservation. In the nineteenth century, Henrik Ibsen presented the problem of the "life-lie" in his drama *The Wild Duck:* there are illusions, he suggested, of which men and women may not be deprived without losing the ability to go on living. Since the turn of the twentieth century, a number of writers have suggested a concept of the "political myth" of a state, which bears a strange resemblance to the "life-lie" discussed by Henrik Ibsen: certain political beliefs, they suggest, must not be subjected to the test of verification, since their disproof might harm political stability. At bottom, this seems the old problem of orthodoxy and heresy, the problem of Dostoevsky's Grand Inquisitor, returned in political garb.

Jaspers' philosophy, like the tragedies of Oedipus and

Hamlet, implies the opposite of this position. Jaspers holds fast to man's commitment to truth, and to the integrity and openness of his search for it, even at the price of failure:

If totally manifest, truth paralyzes — unless man finds a way, as Hamlet does, through desperate heroism and uncorrupted vision, in the restless movement of a shaken soul. . . . Truth, whole and complete — whether as the source of death or of peace — is not available to us in life and time. Within time, truth is forever under way, always in motion and not final even in its most marvellous crystallizations. Never to retreat from this fundamental situation — that is the condition on which alone philosophic thought can remain truthful.

Man thus must face his limits, and, looking back from the outermost border of his strength, understand more clearly his own situation. Some of his limits he can overcome by breaking through them; others he can transcend in his mind by awareness and extrapolation from symbols; at still others he will fail. But even the experience of failure may be crucial. One person's failure may acquire transcending symbolic significance for the thought or conduct of others; and it may lead to new possibilities even for the person who failed — to possibilities of restructuring his own personality and the further pattern of his life.

Essential throughout this philosophic quest is man's will to communication — not merely to the communication of the near, the trite, the obvious, and the agreed-upon, but communication of the difficult, the controversial, and the half-unknown, the matters at the limits of our awareness and our powers. It must be both communication among human beings, and communication as receptivity to the codes and *chiffres* in which finite things suggest information about the unknown but encompassing reality.

Such communication, as Jaspers speaks of it, seems to resemble some aspects of communion. Like communion, it must be open, warm, and unreserved. But unlike communion, it is a philosophic and not a religious act. Philosophic communication must seek to be clear, rational, specific, and articulate. It can be accomplished, therefore, only very incompletely; and the "boundless will to communication," which is a major element of Jaspers' "philosophic faith," denotes not merely this very limited achievement, but rather the ceaseless effort required to attain it.

Tragedy, though rich in truth, is not enough for Karl Jaspers. It is a basic aspect of reality, and we can neither deny nor escape it. But the experience of tragedy is only one stage in man's process of learning. Taken as an absolute, tragic knowledge turns into idolatry, whether it be idolatry of images or idolatry of self. Rather, Jaspers seems to say, men and women must remain open to the voice of the world-wide misery without grandeur that cries out for help, and they must seek to transcend the limits that bound their sensitivity and their ability to help today. All of us, he seems to suggest, must seek the hard way that continues beyond tragedy — the way of which perhaps the Bible speaks when it calls upon men to overcome their limits by being "born again," while yet remaining "members of one another."

KARL W. DEUTSCH

TRAGEDY IS NOT ENOUGH

CHAPTER ONE

Awareness of the Tragic

It is essential to the nature of man that he should look into the depths of truth. Truth is within his reach and within his mind, wherever there is language, however crude and obscure.

Systematic philosophy is a leap forward. But this leap does not invalidate man's earlier awareness of truth. For this awareness contains those original visions that from the beginning of time have prompted man to hand down truth in the form of images, ritual, and legends. At this stage, the power of myth, the authority of revelation, and the disciplined conduct of life are realities. Basic questions are not yet formulated with anything like rational awareness; they find their answers not in the form of logical reflection but in that of accepted fact. Why is man's condition what it is? The Fall from Grace and the myths of Prometheus answer the human problem and at the same time present it anew. How do I achieve purity, redemption, and freedom from fear? Mystery cults, rites, and rules of conduct give answers and point the way.

Historically, philosophy takes shape as systematic

thought during the centuries — 600 to 300 B.C. — in which the language of elemental visions reaches its highest point of clarity, maturity, and power.

Philosophy is inseparable from such visions. It provokes and intensifies the elementary images. And whether it battles to overcome them, or assimilates and utilizes them, they in their turn deeply perplex and affect it. For philosophy sees in such images its own counterpart: they must be either resisted or incorporated and confirmed. In the end, philosophy is left to face a few images which it can in no way understand; and it recognizes these as utterly distinct from itself. Philosophers who continue to deal with these irreducible images, for whatever purpose, will eventually see them evolve into the instruments of philosophic inquiry.

At first these basic conceptions are the one language of truth. They form an all-inclusive and indivisible whole that shapes man's life and makes it complete. It is only in the course of further development that religion, art, and poetry become separated from each other. Such separation splits the language of truth into several branches. Their original unity nevertheless continues to have its effect upon all these branches and keeps them linked.

1. Religion

What was revealed in religion as foundation and as limit, giving strength to both community and individual, remains the predestined area of philosophic inquiry and the basis of its findings. Religion becomes the polar opposite of philosophy. It offers a continuous challenge to philosophic penetration. But the resistance it offers to philosophic efforts turns out to be productive. It was religion that made the soul the very foundation of man's humanity, though subsequently this soul has discarded the specific historical form of religion, thereby seeming to abandon religion itself.

For man, to abandon and forget religion completely would be to end the philosophic quest itself. It would be replaced by unreasoning despair ignorant of itself, a life lived merely from moment to moment, a kind of nihilism full of chaotic superstition. Ultimately, even science would die. Man's fundamental questions — What is man? What can he become? What will become of him? — would no longer reflect serious experience. They would no longer be asked. Of course these same questions would take on new disguises, but they would remain limited to answers which would make human life seem incomprehensible and meaningless.

2. Fine Arts

The fine arts make our visible world speak to us. We see things as art teaches us to see them. We experience space through the form the architect has imposed upon it; we experience a landscape as it has been epitomized in its religious architecture, shaped by human labor, and made a part of life by constant use. We experience nature and man only as they are reduced to their essence in sculpture, drawing, and painting. In a sense, it is when this is done, and only when this is done, that things assume their characteristic form and reveal their visible quality and soul which had previously seemed hidden.

We must distinguish between art as expression of a particular aesthetic ideal and art as a code of symbols for metaphysical reality. The two coincide only when beauty happens to reveal transcendent reality, when such reality is experienced as beautiful, and when everything is seen as essentially beautiful for the reason that it is real. The term "great art" we reserve for metaphysical art — that is to say, an art whose visible creations reveal the underlying reality. It is axiomatic that all representation not so self-transcendent — all mere decoration, all performance which merely charms the senses — can never be more than art in the sense of technical cleverness with no relation to philosophy. This holds true wherever the aesthetic has become divorced from metaphysical contexts.

3. Poetry

Language turns experience into concepts. Within language, poetry is the vocabulary which can communicate everything so discovered. It permeates all expressions of man's nature, from verbal magic accompanying rites of sacrifice, to the invocation of the gods in prayer and hymn, and finally to the representation of human lives and destinies. Poetry is the cradle of language itself, man's first created speech, insight, and action. It is as poetry that philosophy makes its first appearance.

Poetry is the medium through which, in the most natural

and self-evident way, we first apprehend the universe around us and the world within us. When language sweeps us into this current of new experience, we are transformed. Our imagination is aroused by poetry, and imperceptibly it develops within us the whole range of mental images. These alone will enable us to grasp reality firmly.

4. Knowledge of the Tragic: The Insight Gained from Tragedy

At first, as we have seen, religion, art, and poetry were one. What was formulated in their original visions is nothing less than the total content of our consciousness. Consider a single instance from this vast area: tragic fate and deliverance. All the many varieties of tragedy have something in common. Tragedy views in tremendous perspectives all that actually exists and occurs; and in its climax of silence, tragedy suggests and brings to realization the highest possibilities of man.

These tragic visions and perspectives contain a hidden philosophy, for they lend meaning to an otherwise meaningless doom. Although we cannot translate this hidden philosophy into intellectual terms, we can by philosophic interpretation throw it into bolder relief. We acquire this hidden philosophy by re-experiencing its original visions. There can be no substitute for this world of visions. As an organon of philosophy, it is an essential part of philosophic thought. But in finding its own fulfillment, this world of visions goes beyond philosophy, which must reach it once again as something distinct from philosophy itself.

All great expressions of tragic knowledge are cast in the mold of history. In style, theme, and intention, they unmistakably bear the signature of their time. But in its concrete historical form no knowledge can be timeless and universal. In every case, man must acquire it anew to bring its truth to life for himself. The differences in the expressions of tragic knowledge are for us historical facts.

Such differences and contrasts among the historical expressions of the tragic pattern cast light upon one another. What is more, they provide the basis for any knowledge of ourselves.

It is through these differences and contrasts that we apprehend the various degrees of tragic consciousness, the various possibilities of interpreting existence by means of the tragic, and the mainsprings of final deliverance in tragedy. The historical expressions of tragic knowledge provide for us a system of possible approaches to understanding.

5. Historical Survey

Let us recall the great instances of tragic knowledge as they were expressed in vision and artistic form:

(a) Homer; the Edda and Icelandic sagas; heroic legends of all peoples, from Europe to China.

(b) Greek tragedy: Aeschylus, Sophocles, Euripides. Only here tragedy arose as independent poetic genre, all later tragedy being either dependent on or — through Seneca — inspired by it.

(c) Modern tragedy represented by three national figures: Shakespeare, Calderón, Racine.

(d) Lessing; tragedy representing the ideals of German culture: Schiller and, subsequently, the nineteenth century.

(e) Other poetry of awe and terror asking their own questions of the problem of existence: the Book of Job; several Indic dramas (none of which, however, is entirely tragic).

(f) Tragic knowledge in Kierkegaard, Dostoevsky, Nietzsche.

Heroic sagas display the tragic world view as self-evident. This embodies as yet no intellectual struggle with a problem, and as yet no yearning for deliverance. Stark disaster, death and doom, unflinchingness and glory: these are what matter.

Great tragedy, Greek as well as modern, arises in eras of transition: it comes up like a flame from the fires that consume an epoch. It declines in the end to mere decoration.

Greek tragedy is a semi-ritual acting out of man's desperate struggle for knowledge of the gods, the meaning of existence, and the nature of justice. At first it is part of the belief in order and deity, in basic and valid institutions, and in the city-state. In the end it may cast doubt upon all these products of history, but it never questions the Idea of Justice or the reality of Good and Evil (Euripides).

Shakespeare, on the contrary, moves across a purely secular stage; in his dramatic personages a proud society recognizes its own heightened image. Human life understands itself in terms of its potentialities and perils, its greatness and nothingness, its human and diabolical strains, its nobleness and meanness, its sheer joy of being alive and its bewildered terror at failure and destruction, its love, dedication, and openness of heart, and then again its hatred, narrowness, and blindness. All in all, humanity sees itself confronted by an unanswerable problem, by the ultimate collapse of every effort to realize its promise — all this against the background of unshaken order and a strongly felt contrast between Good and Evil.

Calderón and Racine are high points of Christian tragedy. In them tragedy is charged with a new kind of tension. In them, instead of destiny and demons, we have Providence and Grace, even damnation. Instead of the question asked only that it might be answered by ultimate silence, all is now sustained by the certainty of the Beyond and an all-merciful God. Instead of the unceasing struggle for truth, which the poet carries through from one composition to the next, and instead of the play with symbolic ciphers, we now see truth actually present in the knowledge that both the sinful world and God Himself are indeed realities. But within the tensions of this new polarity, the genuinely tragic has become extinguished by Christian Truth. The tragedies of Calderón and Racine, because they are of Christian faith, look to more distant horizons; but compared with Shakespeare they are quite narrow in problem and approach, in poignancy and richness of character, in scope and in freedom of outlook.

Absolute and radical tragedy means that there is no way

out whatsoever. Although it might possibly be found in some of Euripides' plays, it does not become really evident until it appears in nineteenth-century drama. Here, however, the collapse of all but merely aesthetic standards at last takes tragedy into a bottomless pit.

6. *Tragic Knowledge of Existence and Untragic Security*

The greatest chasm separates those civilizations that never achieve tragic knowledge — and consequently its vehicles, tragedy, epic, and novel — from those whose way of life is determined by poignant awareness of the intrinsic part tragedy plays in man's existence.

Looking back, we can see how history was rent asunder by the birth of Tragic Man. His tragic insight need not be the product of a flowering civilization, but may be quite primitive. But, primitive or not, man seems truly awake only when he has such knowledge. For now he will face each realization of his ultimate limits with a new restlessness that drives him beyond them. Nothing that is stable will endure, for nothing that is stable will satisfy him. Tragic knowledge is the first phase of that historical movement which takes place not only in external events but in the depths of man himself.

Pre-tragic knowledge is rounded out, complete, and self-contained. It sees man's suffering, doom, and death. There is deep sorrow in such knowledge, and deep joy. Sorrow becomes accepted as part of the eternal cycle of living and dying, death and resurrection, and everlasting change. A God dying and returning, the seasons of the year celebrated as the occasions of this death and rebirth, these are the basic realities. Nearly everywhere on earth we find mythical conceptions of a mother-goddess as the bringer of life or death; she bears and nurses all, loves and lets ripen — but also takes everything back into her womb, kills without mercy, and destroys in tremendous disasters. But such images of fate are not yet tragic knowledge. They represent no more than man's reassuring knowledge of a mortality in which he feels at home. Essentially this knowledge is unaware of history. Here, everything at all times has the same degree of reality. Nothing strikes man as outstandingly important; everything is equally important. Whatever is present is fully and exhaustively present as that which it is.

Tragic knowledge, on the contrary, contains an element of history. Cyclical patterns are merely its background. The crucial events are unique and are always moving on. They are shaped by irrevocable decisions, and they never recur.

But pre-tragic knowledge is not always superseded by tragic knowledge. It may be possible for pre-tragic knowledge to preserve its own truth intact alongside the tragic outlook of other civilizations. No such tragic outlook develops wherever man succeeds both in achieving a harmonious interpretation of the universe and in actually living in accord with it. That is to a great extent what happened in ancient, especially in pre-Buddhist, China. In such a civilization, all misery, unhappiness, and evil are merely temporary disturbances which never need occur.

There is no horror, rejection, or justification of the ways
of this world — no indictment, only lament. Man is not
torn in desperation: he suffers and even dies with composure. There are no hopeless entanglements, no dark
frustrations; all is basically clear, beautiful, and true. To be
sure, terror and horror are part of experience and are as
familiar to this civilization as to those civilizations awak-
ened to an awareness of the tragic. Yet serenity remains the
dominant mood of life; there is no struggle, no defiance. A
deep awareness of the past connects man with the ancient
foundation of all things. What man seeks here is not any
kind of historical movement, but rather the ever-new re-
establishment of an eternal reality that is both orderly and
good. Wherever the tragic sense appears, something
extraordinary is lost: the feeling of security without the
shadow of tragedy, a natural and sublime humanity, a sense
of being at home in this world, and a wealth of concrete
insights — all of which were real for the Chinese at one
time. The relaxed and serene face of the Chinese still contrasts with the tense and self-conscious expression of
Western man.

7. *Tragic Knowledge in Epic and Drama*

The mythical mind sees the world's basic disharmony
reflected in the multiplicity of gods. No man can do justice
to all of them; somewhere the cult of one god is bound to
offend against that of another; the gods are at war among
themselves, and they use men's destinies as stakes in their
battles. But even the gods are not all-powerful; above

both gods and man, dark Moira holds her sway. The questions "Why?" and "Wherefore?" call forth many answers, depending upon the situation, but provide no single answer. Man may encompass the whole wealth of his environment, the whole range of his potentialities. He experiences the extremes. But he does not strain his every fiber in the search for an inclusive unity, and thus he is not yet committed to seek at any price the answer to his question.

Tragic insight of this early type is found in Homer: in the sheer joy of seeing, in the worship of the gods, and in unquestioned steadfastness and endurance.[1]

This same endurance, this same calm defiance in the face of destiny, becomes deliberate in the *Edda* and sagas, and although it is not so richly drawn as in Homer, it is there more impassioned and boundless.

All these views are like tragic knowledge that is only half-grown. They do not distinguish the various kinds of catastrophe,[1a] nor the last unfathomed depths of tragic failure. The man of the heroic age does not yet crave for liberation of the soul: his soul is content if it can find strength to endure. Somehow his questions stop too soon. He accepts life and death too easily as unproblematic and self-evident. His epic point of view differs from the pre-tragic (as in old China) only in this — that it does not shroud the world's discrepancies in a veil of harmony.

Greek tragedy takes its raw material from this world of myth and epic. But there is a difference. Men no longer bear their tragic knowledge calmly, but pursue their questions ceaselessly. Men ask questions and find answers when they transform the myths themselves. Only now the myths attain their full maturity and depth, but no version of them can henceforth remain stable. Each great tragic poet will recast the myths to suit his purposes. Finally those myths are wholly consumed in man's passionate struggle for truth — in the poet's dialogue with the divine — until nothing remains but their ashes: poetic images that still charm but no longer compel.

The questions of tragedy are already philosophical in substance, but they are still formulated in visual, dramatic terms. They have not yet reached the rational method of philosophy. These are the questions directed to the gods: Why are things the way they are? What is man? What leads him on? What is guilt? What is fate? What are the ordinations valid among men, and where do they come from? What are the gods?

These questions search for a road to gods who are just and good, to the one God. But as man travels along this road, tradition slowly disintegrates. It cannot measure up to the new standards of right, goodness, and omnipotence as they become increasingly rational. Skepticism is the end of this high-minded search that is sustained by the contents of tradition brought to their utmost purity and beauty.

In this dramatic re-examination of tradition — acted out at the sacred festivals in honor of Dionysus — the poet wills and achieves something more than man's earlier delight in the untiring representation of nature, men, and gods. Of that delight Hesiod had sung, praising the Muses:

Aye, though fresh troubles have crazed a man till he knows
nothing but dread and despair, should a singer praise,
as the Muses' servant, the glory of ancient days,
the heroes and blessed gods of Olympus-crest,
the man will forget that he ever was darkly distressed,
such powers of healing to gifts of the Muses belong.[2]

Tragedy wants more: the catharsis of the soul. Admittedly, even Aristotle does not make clear to us just what this catharsis is. This much is certain: it is an experience that touches the innermost being of each man.[3] It makes him more deeply receptive to reality, not merely as a spectator, but as a man who is personally involved. It makes truth a part of us by cleansing us of all that in our everyday experience is petty, bewildering, and trivial — all that narrows us and makes us blind.

8. *Tragedy Transcended in the Philosophic Interpretation of the World and in Revealed Religion*

Tragic knowledge uses myth in these two forms: in the epic, as knowledge that without question accepts as real a world of visual images; in tragedy, as knowledge that asks searching questions about deity. Each of these tragic forms in turn provides a way for man to overcome the tragic itself: the epic is the root of every Enlightenment, with its philosophic interpretation of the world; tragedy is the root of revealed religion. Ultimately, both forms are inadequate.

Neither the pre-Socratics nor Plato, with their speculative testing of reality[4] — a testing which is both the opposite and the complement of tragedy — draws the consequences from man's ultimate awareness of his ignorance,[5] at which the tragic poets gradually arrived. It is left to the sober encyclopedic philosophy of the post-Aristotelian era to draw such consequences and to dissolve the faulty conceptions of God endorsed by tradition.[6] This late philosophy then conceives of the universe as a harmony, whose every dissonance is merely relative.

It relativizes the importance of individual destinies, accepting each man's personality[7] as something unshakable, something which merely acts out its destiny in the world like a part in a play, doing so without identifying itself with the part. Here tragic knowledge has lost its weight; its final attitude to existence is no longer the stubbornness of the unyielding hero or the catharsis of the soul entangled in this world. Rather, tragic knowledge in this last stage becomes Apathy, the indestructible serenity of indifference to suffering.

When brought face to face with tragic knowledge, philosophic Apathy fails to carry liberation far enough. In the first place, Apathy is mere endurance. It may claim for precedent the heroic defiance of mythical times, but it lacks the passion of that defiance; almost empty of content, it shrinks to a mere pinpoint of meaningless self-assertion. In the second place, Apathy remains a theory, however impressive, which can hardly be carried through in practice by the majority of people. It is for these reasons that man, out of his tragic knowledge and philosophic emptiness, yearns for a deeper liberation. This liberation is the promise of revealed religion.

Man wants to be saved, and he is saved. But not entirely of his own doing. He is relieved of the burden of this impossible task. Christ's sacrificial death and Buddha's revelation not merely offer help to man, but actually create for him that power with which he has only to co-operate in order to be free.

The revealed religion of Judaism and Christianity views the discrepancies of life, of man, of all that finds tragic expression, as imbedded in the origin of man: original sin is rooted in Adam's Fall. Redemption springs from Christ's death on the cross. All the things of this world are, as such, corrupt: man is steeped in inescapable guilt before he ever incurs guilt as an individual. He has become involved in the one all-pervading process of incurring guilt and finding salvation. He partakes of both through himself, though not through himself alone. He is guilty already through Original Sin, and he is to be saved through grace. Now, however, he takes his cross upon himself. He no longer merely endures the sorrows of existence, its discrepancies and tearing conflicts [8] — he deliberately chooses them. This is tragedy no longer. The darkness of terror is pierced by the radiance of blessedness and grace.

Seen from this point of view, Christian salvation opposes tragic knowledge. The chance of being saved destroys the tragic sense of being trapped without chance of escape. Therefore no genuinely Christian tragedy can exist. For in Christian plays, the mystery of redemption is the basis and framework of the plot, and the tension of tragic knowledge has been released from the outset with the experience of man's perfection and salvation through grace.

At this point, tragedy loses its compelling character: man is aroused by it, not touched in his innermost being. What is essential to the Christian cannot even emerge in tragedy. What is religious in the specific Christian sense forever escapes poetry, for it can only be realized existentially (through and in living), and it cannot be contemplated as an aesthetic phenomenon. In this sense a Christian is bound to misunderstand, say, Shakespeare: Shakespeare succeeds in making everything the subject of his drama, for under every possible aspect he shows man as he really is. But the specifically religious — and only this — escapes him. When confronted with Shakespeare's dramatic works, the Christian knows, as a matter of deep personal experience, that they do not reveal to him, or even touch upon, the boon that is his through faith. It is only indirectly that Shakespeare seems to the Christian eye to lead up to the experience of faith — in the open, jagged[9] fractures of his work, in what it leaves unresolved, in the tenseness of his characters, and in their straining, unspoken and unconscious, toward the chance of being saved.

The substance of this tragic knowledge must escape the Christian. Nevertheless, this tragic knowledge, if it remains philosophic and develops along purely philosophic lines, is also a way for man to transcend his limitations. It offers a unique form of deliverance, but it is not understood from the Christian point of view, and it loses its content whenever it ends in philosophic Apathy.

Every one of man's basic experiences ceases to be tragic in a Christian context. Guilt becomes *felix culpa,* the "happy fault" — the guilt without which no salvation is possible. Judas' betrayal was necessary for Christ's sacrifice and death, the source of salvation for all believers. Christ is the deepest symbol of failure in this world, yet he is in no sense tragic. In his very failure he knows, fulfills, and consummates.

CHAPTER TWO

Basic Characteristics of the Tragic

The tragic looms before us as an event that shows the terrifying aspects of existence,[1] but an existence that is still human. It reveals its entanglement with the uncharted background of man's humanity.[2] Paradoxically, however, when man faces the tragic, he liberates himself from it. This is one way of obtaining purification and redemption.

Breakdown and failure reveal the true nature of things. In failure, life's reality is not lost; on the contrary, here it makes itself wholly and decisively felt. *There is no tragedy without transcendence.* Even defiance unto death in a hopeless battle against gods and fate is an act of transcending: it is a movement toward man's proper essence, which he comes to know as his own in the presence of his doom.

Where awareness of the tragic has become fundamental to man's awareness of reality, we speak of tragic readiness.[3] But we must distinguish between awareness of the transitoriness of things and genuine awareness of the tragic.

When he thinks of transitoriness, man views the actual events leading up to death, as well as the ephemeral character of all life, as parts of the natural cycle of growth, decay, and renewed growth. He recognizes himself as within nature and identifies himself with it. Here man comes upon a secret that makes him tremble. What is the soul which, independent of the flux of time, knows itself to be immortal, although aware of the finiteness of its worldly existence, aware that it is doomed to pass away in death? Yet, neither this fact of mortality nor this secret of the soul can rightly be termed tragic.

Genuine awareness of the tragic, on the contrary, is more than mere contemplation of suffering and death, flux and extinction. If these things are to become tragic, man must act. It is only then, through his own actions, that man enters into the tragic involvement that inevitably must destroy him. What will be ruined here is not merely man's life as concrete existence, but every concrete embodiment of whatever perfection he sought. Man's mind fails and breaks down in the very wealth of its potentialities. Every one of these potentialities, as it becomes fulfilled, provokes and reaps disaster.

A yearning for deliverance has always gone hand in hand with the knowledge of the tragic. When man encounters the hard fact of tragedy, he faces an inexorable limit. At this limit, he finds no guarantee of general salvation. Rather, it is in acting out his own personality, in realizing his selfhood[4] even unto death, that he finds redemption and deliverance.

He may find this deliverance through his sheer strength to bear the unknown without question, and to endure it with unshakable defiance. This, however, is the mere seed of deliverance, its barest possible form. Or he may find deliverance by opening his eyes to the nature of the tragic process which, brought to light, can purify the mind. Finally, deliverance may already have preceded contemplation of the tragic process in the case where some faith has, from the outset, led life onto the road to salvation. Then, tragedy appears as overcome from the beginning as man transcends to the unseen, to God, the background of all backgrounds.

1. Ways of Interpreting Tragic Knowledge

The meaning of those tragedies that lie before us as the work of poets cannot possibly be reduced to a single formula. These works represent man's labor dealing with his knowledge of the tragic. Situations, events, social forces, religious beliefs, and types of character are the means through which man expresses the tragic.

Every one of the great poems has a meaning which cannot be exhausted by interpretation. They offer no more than directions for interpretation to pursue. Where complete rational interpretation is possible, poetry becomes superfluous — indeed, there has never been truly poetic creation from the very beginning. Where interpretation can make some elements stand out clearly, it heightens their accessibility precisely by virtue of a profound vision that is uncharted, that is not exhaustible by any analysis or interpretation.

In all poems the intellectual construction of the poet

asserts itself. In proportion, however, as the thought emerges as such without being made incarnate in dramatic figures, poetry grows weaker. To that degree, then, the work is generated not by the power of tragic vision but by philosophical preference. This is not to say that thoughts in tragic poetry may not have crucial philosophical significance.

Now that we have reviewed tragic knowledge as a whole, our interpretation must give more searching answers to three problems:

(a) What do the objective aspects of the tragic look like? What is the pattern of tragic existence and of a tragic course of events? How is it conceived in thought? Our interpretation of tragic subjects in poetry will yield the answer.

(b) How do the subjective aspects of the tragic work themselves out? How does the tragic enter into consciousness? How is tragic knowledge achieved and, through it, deliverance and redemption?

(c) What is the meaning of any fundamental interpretation of the tragic?

2. The Tragic as Subject of Poetry

Without trying to define the tragic, we visualize the stark immediacy of tragic events as they have achieved form and expression in poetry.

Our interpretation must hold fast to the content of the poet's original vision, to what already has been expressed and interpreted in his work. Interpretation adds to this vision the meaning which is or might be implied in it, whether or not the poet had explicitly thought of it.

In poetry, tragic consciousness gives body to its own thought: it is only through the tragic mood that we can sense tension and disaster in events affecting us directly or in the world as a whole.[5] Tragedy shows up in battle, in victory and in defeat, in guilt. It is the measure of man's greatness in breakdown and failure. Tragedy reveals itself in man's unconditional will to truth. There it stands revealed as the ultimate disharmony of existence.

3. The Tragic Atmosphere

Life and death, the cycle of blossoming and withering away, the fact of transitoriness, do not yet establish in themselves any tragic atmosphere. The onlooker can calmly contemplate this process in which he is himself included and by which he is sheltered. The tragic atmosphere arises as the strange and sinister fate to which we have been abandoned. There is something alien that threatens us, something we cannot escape. Wherever we go, whatever we see, whatever we hear, there is something in the air which will destroy us, no matter what we do or wish.

This mood occurs in Indic drama as the vision of a world which is the setting of our life, a setting in which we have been abandoned without any protection. Thus, in *Kausika's Wrath:*

> The whole world seems a carrion-ground,
> A plain of corpses slain by Siva's servant, Time.
> The firmament at dusk seems red
> With blood of victims executed.
> Like embers of a pyre
> The feeble sun-disk glows; stars above
> Seem but a boneyard in the sky;
> And, like a skull bleached white,
> Glares the pale moon . . .[5a]

Moods of horror dominate some works of Brueghel and Hieronymus Bosch, as well as Dante's *Inferno*. But this mood is nothing more than foreground. We must look for something deeper, but we cannot find it without first passing through these terrors.

The tragic atmosphere in Greek drama is not the mood of all nature.[6] Rather it is related to particular events, particular human figures, perhaps as the tension that grips everything even prior to any specific deed or occurrence, the tension that warns of doom, though no one yet knows what form the doom will take. Aeschylus' *Agamemnon* gives us an example, and one of singular magnificence.

The tragic mood assumes the many shapes of so-called pessimism and its various pictures of this world, whether in Buddhism or in Christianity, in Schopenhauer or in Nietzsche, in the *Edda* or in the *Nibelungenlied*.

4. Battle and Collision

Truth and reality split apart. In consequence of this split, men must support each other in community, and they must battle in collision. Tragic knowledge sees those battles which are unavoidable. The question for the tragic poet is precisely this: Who is battling whom, and what is really colliding with what?

Immediately, the battle which has found poetic expression is the battle of men against men, or of man against himself. Incompatible needs, duties, motives, and qualities of character are locked in combat. Psychological and sociological analysis seems to make these battles understandable in terms of fact. But the poet sees farther and deeper. It is his task to render tragic knowledge visible, and all these limited realities serve him merely as raw material. Through this raw material he points out what is truly at issue in this conflict. The conflict is now understood according to the interpretations of the antagonists, or of the poet and, through him, the spectator. These interpretations of the battle are themselves realities. For significance so uncovered has always generated the strongest motive power. This significance emerges in the plot of the tragedy.

Such interpretations, when embodied in the work of art itself, are either immanent or transcendent. Tragedy may be immanent, as in a battle between the individual and the universal, or as in a battle of different ways of life that succeed each other in history; or it may be transcendent, as in a battle between men and gods, or as in a battle between the gods themselves.

5. *The Individual and the Universal*

The individual is opposed to universal laws, norms, necessities: untragically, he represents mere willfulness

opposing the law; tragically, he represents the genuine
exception which, though opposing the law, yet has truth
on his side.

General principles are concentrated in the forces of
society, in social stratification, rules, and offices. Hence
society may give rise to tragedy. On the other hand,
general principles may be concentrated in human character
as an imperative of eternal laws which run counter to the
drives and the personality of the individual. Hence there
are also tragedies that arise from character.

Commonly, tragic works based on such interpretations
are poetically weak. Human drives which are entirely
concrete, and general rules which are entirely abstract,
can meet in conflicts that may be rationally developed.
But they do not take visible shape as compelling visions
of the depths of existence. The very transparency of these
alternatives exhausts the problem. Where there is no sense
of the infinite vastness of what is beyond our grasp, all we
finally succeed in conveying is misery — not tragedy. This
is the peculiar predicament of modern tragedy since the
Enlightenment.

6. *The Clash of Ways of Life*

A comprehensive philosophy of history should interpret
the changes in man's condition as a meaningful succession
of historical ways of life; in every epoch these ways of life
account for the general situation and the prevailing patterns of action and thought. They do not replace each
other suddenly. The old is still alive while the new unfolds

itself. The mighty breakthrough of the new is bound at first to fail against the staying power and coherence of the old way of life not yet exhausted. Transition is the zone of tragedy.

According to Hegel, the great heroes of history are tragic figures in this sense. They embody the new idea, purely and uncompromisingly. They arise in sunlike splendor. Their real significance goes unnoticed at first, until the old way of life senses its danger and gathers all its forces to destroy the new in the form of its outstanding representative. Whether Socrates or Julius Caesar, the first victorious protagonist of the new principle becomes, at the same time, the victim at the border of two eras. The old is justified in asserting itself, for it still functions; it is still alive and proves itself through its rich and elaborate traditional patterns of life, even though the seed of decay has already begun its fatal germination. The new is justified also, but it is not yet protected by an established social order and culture. For the time being it is still functioning in a vacuum. But it is only the hero, the first great figure of the new way of life, whom the old, in a last frantic rally of all its forces, can destroy. Subsequent breakthroughs, now untragic, will succeed. Plato and Augustus Caesar are brilliantly triumphant; they realize the vision; they mold men through their works; they shape the future. But they live with their gaze fixed upon the first hero who was the victim.

This interpretation represents a particular philosophy of history. It sets out to speculate only about what is immanent in this world, but proceeds to assign substance and personality to historic units which actually cannot be verified. It ends by endowing historical patterns with quasi-demonic self-direction.

7. *Men Against Gods*

The battle takes place between the single individual and the "powers," between man and demons, between man and the gods. These powers are elusive. They escape man if he would grasp or just understand them. They are both there and not there. The same god is helpful and vicious.

Man does not know. Unknowingly and unconsciously he falls prey to the very powers that he wanted to escape.

Man rebels against the gods, as Hippolytus, the chaste youth in the service of Artemis, revolted against Aphrodite. He is overcome in battle with the unconquerable one.

8. *Gods Against One Another*

The battle is a collision of the powers, of the gods themselves: man is only a pawn in these terrible games, or their scene, or their medium; but man's greatness consists precisely in his act of becoming such a medium. By this act, he becomes imbued with a soul and identical with the powers.

In the *Antigone* of Sophocles, the hidden gods of chthonic or political origin are basically such powers locked in mutual combat. But in Aeschylus' *Eumenides* the battles of the gods are quite manifest and in the foreground, determining the needs of men. In the *Prometheus* such battles are represented even without man's entering upon the scene.

Tragic world views always contain evidence of struggles. But is struggle tragic in and for itself? Or if not, what makes it tragic? To decide this question, we must explore further aspects of the tragic world view.

9. Victory and Defeat

Who or what conquers in tragedy? Men and the powers are colliding. The outcome suggests decision in favor of the conqueror: the losers are wrong. But this is not true. Rather, we discover the following aspects of the tragic:

(a) Victory is not his who triumphs but his who fails in defeat. In suffering failure, the loser conquers. The apparent victor is in truth inferior; his victory is fleeting and hollow.

(b) *What conquers is the universal*, the world order, the moral order, the universal laws of life, the timeless — but the very recognition of such universality implies its rejection: the nature of the universal is such that it must crush this human greatness which opposes it.

(c) *In reality nothing conquers*. Instead, everything becomes questionable, the hero as well as the universal. Compared with the *transcendent*, all is finite and relative, and therefore deserves to be destroyed, the particular as well as the universal, the exception as well as the rule. Both the exceptional man and the sublime order have their own limits, beyond which they break down. What conquers in tragedy is the transcendent — or rather even this does not conquer, for it makes itself felt only through the whole situation. It neither dominates nor submits; it simply exists.

(d) In victory and in defeat, in the very process of achieving a solution, a new historical order is born, transitory in its turn. Its significance applies first to the particular knowledge of the tragic from which it arose. The rank of a tragic poet is then determined by the content which he draws from victory and defeat, and from their resolution.

10. Guilt

Tragedy becomes self-conscious by understanding the fate of its characters as the consequence of guilt, and as the inner working out of guilt itself. Destruction is the atonement of guilt.

To be sure, the world is full of guiltless destruction. Hidden evil destroys without being seen; it acts without being heard; no worldly authority so much as hears about it, any more than when someone was being tortured to death in the dungeon of a castle. Men die as martyrs without being martyrs, in so far as no one is present to bear witness or to learn of their martyrdom. Every day some defenseless creatures are being tortured and destroyed on this earth. Ivan Karamazov flies into a mad rage at the thought of the children killed for mere pleasure by the warring Turks. But this whole heart-rending, gruesome reality is not tragic, in so far as disaster is not the atonement of a guilt and is unconnected with the meaning of this life.

The question of guilt, however, is not limited to the actions and lives of individual men. Rather, it refers to humanity as a whole, of which every one of us is a part. Where are we to look for the guilt that is responsible for all this undeserved disaster? Where is the power that makes the innocent miserable?

Wherever men saw this question clearly, they conceived of the idea of complicity in guilt. All men are jointly committed and jointly liable. Their common origin and their common goal account for this. A token of this, though not an explanation, is that we feel shaken and perplexed[7] at the following thought, which seems absurd to our limited understanding: I am responsible for all the evil that is perpetrated in the world, unless I have done what I could to prevent it, even to the extent of sacrificing my life. I am guilty because I am alive and can continue to live while this is happening. Thus criminal complicity takes hold of everyone for everything that happens.

We must therefore speak of guilt in the wider sense of a guilt of human existence as such,[8] and of guilt in the narrower sense of responsibility for any particular action. Where our own guilt is not limited to certain specific wrongdoings but, in a deeper sense, is found in the very nature of human existence, there the idea of guilt becomes truly inclusive. Tragic knowledge, therefore, distinguishes these two kinds of guilt:

First: Existence is guilt. Guilt in the larger sense is identical with existence as such. The idea, already found in Anaximander, recurs in Calderón, although in a different sense — that man's greatest guilt is to have been born.

This is revealed also in the fact that my very existence

causes misery. Indian thought has an image for this: with every step, with every breath, I destroy living beings. Whether I act or not, merely by existing I infringe upon the existence of others. Passive or active, I incur the guilt of existence.

A particular life is guilty through its origin. True, I did not desire this world nor my particular existence in it. But I am guilty against my will, simply because it is I myself who have this origin. My descent from guilty ancestors causes my own guilt.

Antigone is born contrary to the law as the daughter of Oedipus and his own mother. The curse of her descent is active within her. But her very exclusion from the norm of legitimate descent accounts for her singular depth and human feeling: she possesses the surest and most unshakable knowledge of the divine law. She dies because she is greater than the others, because her exceptional case embodies truth. And she dies gladly. Death to her means release; all along her road of action she is at one with herself.

A particular character is guilty because of what he is.[9] Character is itself a form of destiny — in so far as I detach myself from my own character and turn to look upon it.

What baseness there is in me, what desires to do evil, what unregenerate pride there is in my perversity — all this I myself have neither wanted nor created. Yet I am guilty of all this. And my guilt begets my destiny, whether I die unwillingly and unredeemed, or whether I am destroyed in trying to transcend my base nature by summoning up a deeper resource of my being — a resource which enables me to reject what I was, even though I cannot become what I long to be.

Second: Action is guilt. Guilt in the narrower sense is found in any distinct action I carry out freely in the sense that it need not occur and could also occur differently.

Guilty action may consist in flouting the law; it is personal arbitrariness consciously opposing the universal for no other reason than its own arbitrariness. It is the consequence of culpable ignorance, of half-conscious transpositions and concealments of motives. Nothing else is involved in such willfulness beyond the misery of meanness and evil.

The situation is different when tragic knowledge recognizes the guilt of an action. Truthful and morally necessary action, although springing from the foundation of freedom, may entail failure. Man cannot escape his guilt through right and truthful conduct: guilt itself seems incurred guiltlessly. Man takes this guilt upon himself. He does not try to evade it. He stands by his guilt, not out of personal stubbornness, but for the sake of the very truth, which is destined for failure in his necessary sacrifice.[10]

11. Man's Greatness in Failure

Tragic knowledge cannot be extended and deepened without seeing in man the quality of greatness over and above his atonement of guilt.

That man is not God is the cause of his smallness and undoing. But that he can carry his human possibilities to their extreme and can be undone by them with his eyes open — that is his greatness.

What we essentially learn from tragic knowledge, therefore, is what makes man suffer and what makes him fail, what he takes upon himself in the face of which realities, and in what manner or form he sacrifices his existence.

The tragic hero — man heightened and intensified — is man himself in good and evil, fulfilling himself in goodness and canceling out his own identity in evil.[11] In each case his existence is shipwrecked by the consistency with which he meets some unconditional demand, real or supposed.

His resistance, stubbornness, and pride drive him into the "greatness" of evil. His endurance, his dauntlessness, his love, raise him up into the good. Always he grows in stature through the experience of life at its limits. The poet sees in him the bearer of something that reaches beyond individual existence, the bearer of a power, a principle, a character, a demon.

Tragedy depicts a man in his greatness beyond good and evil. The poet's view resembles that of Plato: "Or do you suppose that great crimes and unmixed wickedness spring from a slight nature and not from a vigorous one . . . while a weak nature will never be the cause of anything great, either for good or for evil?" It is from the most gifted type of man that "these spring who do the greatest harm to communities and individuals, and the greatest good . . . , but a small nature never does anything great for a man or a city."[12]

CHAPTER THREE

The Problem of Truth

Tragedy occurs wherever the powers that collide are true independently of each other. That reality is split, that truth is divided, is a basic insight of tragic knowledge.

Hence the question animating tragedy is: What is true? And, following from it: Who is right? Is the right cause successful in this world? Does truth conquer? To reveal some particular truth in every agent and at the same time the limitations of this truth, and so to reveal the injustice in everything — this indeed is the process of tragedy.

But then, in several tragedies (such as *Oedipus* and *Hamlet*), the hero himself is asking for the truth. The very possibility of truth becomes dramatic subject matter, and with it the whole problem of knowledge, its very possibility, as well as its meaning and its consequences.

In our interpretation of these two inexhaustible tragedies we shall lay stress on this basic problem.

1. Oedipus

Oedipus is the man who wills to know. He is the superior, thinking solver of riddles who conquers the Sphinx. Because of this, he becomes ruler of Thebes. He is the man, unwilling ever to use deceit, who brings to light the horrible deeds he has unknowingly committed. Thereby he effects his own destruction. He is fully aware of the blessing and the curse of his quest, seizing both because he wants the truth.

Oedipus is guiltless. He does everything within his power to avoid committing the evil deeds the oracle has prophesied — that he should commit parricide and should marry his mother. He avoids the country of those who he thinks are his parents. Unknowingly, then, in another country, he kills his real father and marries his mother. "None of this I did willingly." "I did it unknowingly and without guilt before the law."[1]

The tragedy shows how Oedipus as the ruler of Thebes tries to keep the threatening plague away from his country: unsuspectingly at first, he searches for the cause of the evil, then recoils in premonition, and finally and inexorably brings the truth to light.

The oracle tells Oedipus his father's murderer is still at large in the country: he must be expelled if the plague is to be turned away. But who is the murderer? Teiresias the seer is consulted and will not reply: "Alas, how dreadful to have wisdom where it profits not the wise." "You are all ignorant. No. I will never tell you what I know. Now it is my misery; then, it would be yours."[2]

Oedipus urges him, insults him, forces him to talk, and at last learns that he himself is the offender who has desecrated the land. Perplexed by this impossibility, Oedipus mocks the seer's knowledge and invokes his own, rationally grounded as it is, which has enabled him rather than the seer to vanquish the Sphinx, "guessing the truth by mother-wit, not bird-lore."[3]

But the seer, now provoked to the utmost, hints at the terrible truth by questions: "You . . . mock my blindness. Have you eyes, and do not see your own damnation? . . . Whose son are you?"[4]

Now Oedipus starts searching. By questioning his mother he learns the truth of the situation: a man may strive to know, may excel at inquiry and in knowledge — and yet may unknowingly commit the worst of crimes. Life and happiness may flourish, nonetheless, until these in turn are utterly destroyed by knowledge — that is the maze of truth and life that rests unsolved:

> Then would not he speak aright of Oedipus, who judged
> these things sent by some cruel power above man?[5]

Recoiling from the full truth, Oedipus wishes to die rather than finally have to face it:

> May I be gone out of men's sight before
> I see the deadly taint of this disaster
> come upon me.[6]

In vain Jocasta tries to steer him back into the unquestioning ignorance that makes life possible:

> Why should man fear since chance is all in all
> for him, and he can clearly foreknow nothing?
> best to live lightly, as one can, unthinkingly.
> As to your mother's marriage bed, — don't fear it.

> Before this, in dreams too, as well as oracles,
> many a man has lain with his own mother.
> But he to whom such things are nothing bears
> his life most easily. . . .
> I beg you — do not hunt this out . . .[7]

But nothing can move Oedipus to veil the truth again, once he has discerned some features of it: "I must. I cannot leave the truth unknown."[8]

When he has uncovered the truth he tears out his own eyes. Henceforth they are to stare into night because they failed to "behold such horrors as I was suffering and working!"[9]

The chorus draws its conclusion in a way applicable to the whole of man's life; life is illusion, disillusionment is destruction:

> Alas, ye generations of men, how mere a shadow do I count your life! Where, where is the mortal who wins more of happiness than just the seeming, and, after the semblance, a falling away? Thine is a fate that warns me, — thine, thine, unhappy Oedipus — to call no earthly creature blest.[10]

With his thirst for knowledge and his superior understanding, Oedipus always travels an unintended road. He falls prey to the disaster of knowledge, a disaster he had never suspected: "Thou cursed through knowledge and through fate!"[11]

But this unrelenting thirst for knowledge and the unconditional acceptance of its consequences all the way to disaster — these create another truth. A new value is divinely bestowed upon Oedipus, he who had been cursed through knowledge and through fate. His bones confer blessings upon the land where he is laid to rest. Men care for his remains and make his grave a hallowed place. Oedipus himself has achieved an inner reconciliation, and this at last finds outward expression: his tomb becomes a shrine.

2. Hamlet [12]

An unprovable crime has been committed. The king of Denmark has been murdered by his brother, who has then taken the throne himself and married the slain man's wife. A ghost has revealed this to Hamlet, the murdered king's son, alone, without any witnesses. No one except the criminal himself — the new king — knows of the crime. In the present state of Denmark no one told of the murder would believe it had occurred. The ghost, because he is a ghost, cannot be a conclusive witness for Hamlet. The crime itself cannot be proved, though Hamlet senses it, almost as if he knew. Hamlet's life is now dedicated to a single task: to prove the unprovable, and, after proof, to act.

The whole play is the drama of Hamlet's search for truth. But truth is not only the answer to the bare question of the facts of the case. It is more. The state of the entire world is such that this crime could take place, that it could remain undetected, that it still eludes clarification. The moment that Hamlet realizes his task, he also knows that:

> The time is out of joint. O cursed spite
> That ever I was born to set it right! [13]

Any man in Hamlet's place, knowing what no one knows and yet not knowing it for sure, sees all the world in a new and different light. He keeps to himself what he cannot communicate. Every human being, every situation, every ordinance stands revealed as in itself untrue through its resistance to the search, its subservience to a conspiracy against the truth. There is a flaw in everything. Even the best-intentioned among the good fail in their own way (Ophelia, Laertes). "To be honest, as this world goes, is to be one man picked out of ten thousand."[14]

Hamlet's knowledge and his desire for knowledge set him apart from the world. In it, he cannot be of it. He acts the part of a madman. In this counterfeit world, madness is the mask which allows him not to lie about his real feelings, not to feign respect where he feels none. He can speak the truth through irony. Whatever he say, true or untrue — equivocal for all — he can cover with the mask of madness. He chooses madness as his proper role because truth admits of no other.

The instant Hamlet realizes that he is marked as an exception and is fated to exclusion, he is shocked into full recognition of what is happening to him. He addresses his friends as if he were taking leave of all possible sheltered human existence — yet at the same time he conceals from them that this is his farewell:

> I hold it fit that we shake hands and part;
> You, as your business and desire shall point you,
> For every man hath business and desire,
> Such as it is; and for my own poor part,
> Look you, I'll go pray.[15]

But the mask assumed is only a disguise in daily life. Hamlet must assume an actual role, that of the seeker for truth in a world radically untrue, the role of avenger of the crime committed. This role cannot be carried through without equivocation, impurity, distortion. Hamlet must take upon himself the agony of the tension between his nature and the role assigned him, until he can no longer see himself as he is but must reject himself as someone warped and twisted. This alone explains his judgments on himself.

Many interpreters have pictured Hamlet as a man unable to make up his mind, nervous, hesitating, and ever late — an inactive dreamer. Many self-accusations seem to confirm such an opinion:

> Yet I,
> A dull and muddy-mettled rascal, peak,
> Like John-a-dreams . . .[16]

> Thus conscience does make cowards of us all;
> And thus the native hue of resolution
> Is sicklied o'er with the pale cast of thought;
> And enterprises of great pith and moment
> With this regard their currents turn awry,
> And lose the name of action . . .[17]
> How all occasions do inform against me
> And spur my dull revenge! . . .
>   . . . or some craven scruple
> Of thinking too precisely on th' event —
> A thought which, quarter'd, hath but one part wisdom
> And ever three parts coward, — I do not know
> Why yet I live to say "This thing's to do,"
> Sith I have cause, and will, and strength, and means
> To do't.[18]

Indeed, Hamlet must appear inactive; he continually finds a reason for not acting. And he strikes himself that way. He speaks every one of the words above in order to drive himself to action.

But that precisely is the basic characteristic of the tragedy. Hamlet is always in action; he is forever seeking the goal of truth and the conduct that will correspond to it. His reasons for hesitating are entirely and thoroughly justified if measured by the yardstick of what is actually true. It is the situation forced upon him by fate that makes him appear a weakling paralyzed by reflection.

Hamlet is in no sense cowardly or irresolute. Rather, the opposite manifests itself again and again:

> I do not set my life at a pin's fee . . .[19]

He risks his life with temerity wherever he makes his appearance. He has presence of mind and instantly hits upon the proper decisions (for example, in dealing with Rosencrantz and Guildenstern). He is superior to all; he is bold, and able to fight with his sword as well as with his wit. It is not his character that paralyzes him. Only the predicament of a man who knows — with a sovereign command of penetrating vision — yet does not know, makes him linger. When for an instant his temper sweeps him away in a supreme outburst of passion and he kills Polonius, thinking him the king, he still is in no sense at one with his own violence, not even if the king had been his victim. For the meaning of his task requires not merely that the king should be killed by some avenger; the real task is for someone to demonstrate convincingly just what this king has done. Compared with the average so-called man of determination who rushes into action with blind impulsiveness, Hamlet indeed does not act, at any rate not with unthinking immediacy. He is, as it were, caught up in his knowledge, and in the knowledge of his ignorance. On the other hand, those who have nothing but determination in their forceful assurance, their unthinking obedience, their unquestioning brutality — they are in reality caught up in the narrowness of their illusions. Only a dull-witted enthusiasm for that drastic and immediate resort to action which characterizes men passively subservient to their impulses could accuse Hamlet of inactivity.

The opposite is true. The instant he first saw his task clearly, Hamlet said:

> My fate cries out
> And makes each petty artery in this body
> As hardy as the Nemean lion's nerve.[20]

This commitment he kept unto the very last, right through his quick turns of decision in the fatal duel with Laertes. Every shade of the play reveals Hamlet's tension between clearest vision and active commitment in a single movement toward his goal. It is interrupted only once, by the stabbing of Polonius, a blind deed of impulse, not one of clear vision. Action and mask, however, do not in themselves constitute the whole truth. This truth is realized only as deed and mask are revealed to Hamlet's contemporaries, at whom his will is aimed — those who must make this truth part of their knowledge. This is confirmed in Hamlet's last words to Horatio, who wants to die with him:

> O good Horatio, what a wounded name,
> Things standing thus unknown, shall live behind me!
> If thou didst ever hold me in thy heart,
> Absent thee from felicity awhile,
> And in this harsh world draw thy breath in pain,
> To tell my story.[21]

Hamlet's fate is a riddle to which there is no answer. It is the story of a man whose will to truth is without limit; but it cannot point out the just, the good, and the true as such. The drama ends in silence. And yet some fixed points stand out. They are not in themselves the whole truth, but Hamlet endorses them in the course of his destiny; they are guideposts not for himself but, through him, for others. His affirmation of this world manifests itself as his affirmation of the men who belong to him in his tragedy, and through their contrast they once more raise his exceptional character and fate to almost unscalable heights.

Horatio is Hamlet's only friend, a man truthful and loyal, able to endure, ready to die, one whom Hamlet can address in these words:

> Since my dear soul was mistress of her choice,
> And could of men distinguish, her election
> Hath sealed thee for herself. For thou hast been
> As one, in suff'ring all, that suffers nothing;
> A man that Fortune's buffets and rewards
> Hast ta'en with equal thanks; and blest are those
> Whose blood and judgment are so well commingled
> That they are not a pipe for Fortune's finger

> To sound what stop she please. Give me that man
> That is not passion's slave, and I will wear him
> In my heart's core, ay, in my heart of heart,
> As I do thee. Something too much of this![22]

Horatio is related to Hamlet in nature and character. But task and destiny lead Hamlet on the lonely path of a fundamental experience that he can share with no one.

Fortinbras is a man who lives and acts unquestioningly under the simple illusion of this world's reality. He acts without anxiety. He stresses honor. After Hamlet's death he simply states:

> For me, with sorrow I embrace my fortune.
> I have some rights of memory in this kingdom,
> Which now to claim my vantage doth invite me.[23]

He at once makes use of what has happened, but he respects with quiet shock the fate of the dead prince. In ordering the highest honors to be paid him, Fortinbras once more confirms Hamlet's quality, as it would have shown itself to the world from Denmark's throne:

> For he was likely, had he been put on,
> To have prov'd most royally.[24]

Fortinbras, that ignorant realist unaware of his ignorance, can live. His strength is of the finite kind, limited to the natural purposes of his position, unaware of the hopelessness of a merely finite existence. As for this world's finite purposes, Fortinbras enjoys the confidence of Hamlet, the clear-sighted: "He has my dying voice."[25]

Still, despite Fortinbras's nobility, his life dedicated only to honor is limited and false. This was expressed earlier when Hamlet compared himself with Fortinbras:

> Rightly to be great
> Is not to stir without great argument,
> But greatly to find quarrel in a straw
> When honour's at the stake . . .
>   . . . while to my shame I see
> The imminent death of twenty thousand men
> That for a phantasy and trick of fame
> Go to their graves like beds . . .[26]

Hamlet can be neither Horatio nor Fortinbras. Does he himself lack all possibility of fulfillment? Hamlet's quest for truth with the terror of its final resolution seems to allow him no self-realization except in a negative sense. The poet only once allows Hamlet to conceive, if but for a moment, of a chance for self-realization. That is when, full of confidence, he writes to Ophelia:

> Doubt thou the stars are fire;
>   Doubt that the sun doth move;
> Doubt truth to be a liar;
>   But never doubt I love.[27]

By an absolute standard Hamlet experiences inside himself something unshakable, something that is more than truth. For even truth can be deceptive, whatever its appearance: that is the theme of this tragedy. But Ophelia fails him. Hamlet's one chance vanishes in this most dreadful of his soul's disruptions.

Hamlet's way to truth presents no salvation. There is an area of ignorance, a constant awareness of limits, surrounding his fate. And beyond the limits is there nothingness? That these limits do not border upon nothingness is quietly suggested throughout the play, in hints which seem to carry everything.

Hamlet refuses to give in to superstition — he refuses not only from clarity of knowledge, but also from confidence in something unspecified yet all-encompassing:

> We defy augury; there's a special providence in the fall of a sparrow. If it be now, 'tis not to come. . . . The readiness is all. Since no man knows aught of what he leaves, what is't to leave betimes?[28]

And with an even more deliberate view toward concrete action:

> . . . let us know,
> Our indiscretion sometimes serves us well
> When our deep plots do pall; and that should learn us
> There's a divinity that shapes our ends,
> Rough-hew them how we will . . .[29]

The ways in which Hamlet speaks of his ignorance do not point to nothingness but to transcendence:

> There are more things in heaven and earth, Horatio,
> Than are dreamt of in your philosophy.[30]

The attitude of ignorance seems charged with incomprehensible meaning when the ghost, appearing to Hamlet, refuses to speak further:

> But this eternal blazon must not be
> To ears of flesh and blood.[31]

And, in Hamlet's last words, "The rest is silence."[32]

After all this restraint and indirection, Horatio sets the seal on the story with his moving words to his dead friend:

> Now cracks a noble heart. Good night, sweet prince,
> And flights of angels sing thee to thy rest![33]

To none other, perhaps, of his dying heroes has Shakespeare given such a farewell. To be sure, when compared with such recurrent types as the Stoic sage, the Christian saint, and the Indian hermit, Hamlet does not provide the model for any widely followed form of life. But he remains unique as the truly noble man, unwavering in his will to truth and to sublime humanity. He enters wholly into this world; he does not withdraw from it, but finds the world excluding him. He is unique in his utter self-abandonment to fate, in his heroism without pathos.

It is the predicament of man which achieves expression in the parables of the play *Hamlet*. Can truth be found? Is it possible to live with truth? The condition of man supplies an answer to this question: All life-force stems from blindness. It grows from imagined knowledge, in myth taken for faith, and in the substitute myths; in unquestioning acceptance, and in mind-narrowing untruths. Within the human predicament the quest for truth presents an impossible task.

If totally manifest, truth paralyzes — unless man finds a way, as Hamlet does, through desperate heroism and uncorrupted vision, in the restless movement of a shaken soul. Reflective thought — rational consciousness — enfeebles man, unless the unbroken drive of a personality gathers even more strength in the clear light of knowledge. But such a drive consumes itself without concrete fulfillment, leaving an impression of greatness superhuman — not inhuman — in its failure. This is also confirmed from other points of view. Thus Nietzsche understood that man can never fully accept truth, that to err is necessary — that is, he must err in regard to the fundamental truths which in every case are the premises of his existence. Or again, Hölderlin has Empedocles offend the gods by trying to reveal the whole truth to the people. It is forever the same question: Must man die of truth? Does truth spell death?

The tragedy of Hamlet represents man's knowledge trembling at the edge of destruction. There is in it no warning, no moralizing, only a man's knowledge of fundamental reality in his awareness of his ignorance and in his will to truth, whereby his life is shattered: "The rest is silence."

CHAPTER FOUR

The Subjectivity of the Tragic

Tragic knowledge is not a matter for the unconcerned spectator, interested only in cognition. Rather it is a gaining of knowledge wherein I grow in selfhood by the very manner in which I think I am achieving understanding, by the way in which I see and feel. In and through this knowledge, the whole man is transformed. This transformation may go the way of deliverance, where man rises to supreme reality through conquest of the tragic. Otherwise this transformation may go the way of decline into the irresponsible aestheticism of the spectator: man distracted, drifting, falling off into nothingness.

1. The Concept of Deliverance [1]

Abandoned to this world and all its misery, with no escape from threatening disaster, man reaches out for deliverance, for help in this world or for salvation in the world to come, for liberation from present anguish or for redemption from all distress.

Each man is saved by taking practical action within his own situation, together with his companion. But above and beyond such activity, help has been supplied since time immemorial by certain individuals, specially endowed or possessed as magicians, shamans, or priests, through methods accessible only to them.

The last millennium B.C. marks a deep division in the history of man. Human consciousness conceives the universal character of distress and finds deliverance and redemption through prophets and saviors. These men turn to man as man, their claim is universal, they offer help to all. No longer is distress merely a matter of daily existence, merely a matter of sickness, old age, and death; now it connotes a fundamental bondage of man *as* man and of the world (through ignorance; through sin; through disorder). Saviors, peace makers, and architects of world order, then, no longer provide some particular worldly aid for the moment. They do more than that. With such partial help — or even without it — they show the way to deliverance as a whole.

Such redemption consists in objective events made known to man through revelation, thereby enabling him to know the right way within the whole, and within it to chart the right path for himself.

The world process may be imagined in two distinct ways. Unhistorically, it can be thought of as cyclical recurrence. Historically, it can be understood as something unique, marked by the great and decisive events of collapse and recovery, and by the successive strides of revelation. In either case, however, the world process has a universal and transcending character: it transcends all particular events, whether these are general laws governing a cycle or whether they form some non-repetitive course of general history. Cyclical or historical, the world process transcends itself, and the conscious experience of its uncharted background is the basis of redemption. Out of this experience, all distress and anguish are understood and overcome. The individual partakes of this process through discipline and asceticism, and through mystic operations of his consciousness. He is lifted up through grace, through a rebirth of his inner nature in an act of metamorphosis.

Deliverance always connotes more than help in this or that particular misfortune. Out of the experience of fundamental reality, misery itself and liberation from it are experienced as a metaphysical process.

2. Tragedy and Deliverance

The tragic point of view sees human need and suffering as anchored in metaphysics. Without such a metaphysical basis, we have only misery, grief, misfortune, mishap, and failure. The tragic, however, is visible only to a kind of knowledge that transcends all these.

Poetry depicting only horror as such, only brutality, murder, intrigue — in short, everything terrible — is not, by that token, tragic. For in tragedy the hero should have the knowledge of the tragic and the spectator should be led to share in it. This is the origin of the quest for deliverance from the tragic, the quest for fundamental reality.

This question is different for the tragic hero who actually stands at the edge of doom,[2] and for the spectator who

experiences it only as a possibility. The spectator partakes
only through identification. What might befall him, too,
he experiences as if it had already befallen him in fact.
For he has merged his own identity with that larger self
of man which unites him with everyone else. I am myself
inside the human beings represented in the tragedy. To me
the suffering addresses its message: "This is you." "Sympathy" makes man human — sympathy, not in the sense
of vague regrets, but as felt personal involvement: hence
the atmosphere of humaneness found in great tragedy. But
just because the spectator himself is, in point of fact, quite
safe, his serious concern as a human being can easily degenerate into inhuman enjoyment of horror and cruelty,
or into moral self-righteousness, or — by identification
with noble heroes — into self-deception with cheap senti-
ments of unwarranted self-esteem.

Tragic knowledge is consummated in the person of the
protagonist. Not only does he suffer misery, ruin, and
destruction, but he suffers them knowingly. Not only
does he know that he suffers, but his very soul is torn in
the process. Tragedy shows man as he is transformed at
the edge of doom. Like Cassandra, the tragic hero compre-
hends the tragic atmosphere. Through his questions he
relates himself to destiny. In struggle he becomes aware
of that power for which he stands, that power which is yet
not everything. He experiences his guilt and puts questions
to it. He asks for the nature of truth and in full consciousness acts out the meaning of victory and of defeat.

When we watch tragedy, we transcend the limits of

existence and are thereby liberated. Within the knowledge of the tragic the striving for deliverance no longer signifies exclusively the urge to be saved from anguish and misery. It also signifies our urge to be delivered from the tragic structure of reality by transcending that reality. There is, however, a radical difference between deliverance achieved *within* the tragic, and deliverance *from* the tragic. Either the tragic remains intact, and man liberates himself by enduring it and transforming himself within it, or else tragedy itself is, so to speak, redeemed; it ceases to be; it becomes past. Man had to journey through it, but what was tragic has now been penetrated, abolished[3] on its old level; yet fundamentally it is preserved and made the foundation of real life which is now no longer tragic. Whether within the tragic or whether in transcending it, man's blind confusion is followed by deliverance. He does not drown in darkness and chaos, but comes to rest on the firm ground of a reality that is certain and therefore satisfying. But this reality is not unequivocal. For it was gained only by the risk of radical despair. This despair remains as threat and as possibility.

3. Deliverance Within the Tragic

In the face of tragedy the spectator experiences his own deliverance. He is no longer essentially motivated by mere curiosity, the desire to destroy, the itch for stimulation and excitement. All of these are symptoms of something more basic that overcomes man when he is face to face with the tragic. As the spectator is aroused, and led on by an insight that grows as he watches, he encounters fundamental reality and finds in it meaning and stimulus for the ethic of his own life. Through this experience of something universal in his own person, the spectator certainly is liberated, once tragedy has taken complete hold of him. Precisely what this hold is has been explained in a number of ways, all of them important, but none of them adequate, singly or even jointly, to the reality of this compelling experience of tragic insight into the fundamentals of existence:

(a) Watching the tragic hero, man recognizes his own potentiality: he can stand fast no matter what happens.

When a hero stands the test of doom, he gives proof of man's dignity and greatness. Man can be brave and, unshaken in any transformation, can reconstitute himself as long as he lives. And he can sacrifice himself.

Where all meaning disappears, and all certainty vanishes, something arises deep inside man: the self-preservation of his essential identity. This identity preserves itself through endurance — "I have to meet my destiny in silence" — and through the courage to live and the courage, at the limits of the possible, to die with dignity. There is no objective way of calculating when one rather than the other is justified. At first sight, the will to live at any price can seem like so much vital stubbornness. And yet it may be the sign of obedience to hold out at one's assigned station as a matter of course, without doubt and without question. Conversely, to flee from life may at first look like fear. But it can be courageous to seek death where

one is to be forced into a life without dignity and where
only fear of death could make one cling to it.

But what is courage? It is not mere vitality, the energy
of bare defiance. It can consist only in freedom from the
fetters of existence, in that ability to die which to the in-
trepid soul reveals, together with its steadfastness, reality.
Courage is something held in common by all men in so far
as they are men, regardless of their difference in beliefs.
Something elemental is here made manifest: when the
tragic hero freely chooses his doom and perishes a free
man, he reveals to the spectators what each of them
could be.

Face to face with tragedy, the spectator can anticipate,
realize, or strengthen those of his own potentialities that
tragic knowledge has made clear to him.

(b) By watching the doom of what is finite, man witnesses the reality and truth of the infinite. Being is the
background of all backgrounds; it dooms to failure every
particular configuration. The more grandiose the hero and
the idea he is living with, the more tragic the march of
events and the more fundamental the reality that is revealed.

Tragedy is not intended to evaluate morally the justice
of the doom of a guilty man who never ought to have become guilty. Crime and punishment are a narrower framework submerged in moralism. It is only when man's moral
substance articulates itself into powers which collide that
man grows to heroic stature; it is only then that his crime
is reduced to a guiltless and necessary result of his charac-

ter, and it is only then that his doom becomes his restoration, in which the past is included and redeemed.[4] Tragic doom ceases to be meaningless accident and becomes necessity precisely because the absolute has from the outset condemned everything finite. Then the comprehensive reality of the whole process becomes clear — the process for which the individual sacrifices himself precisely because he is great. The tragic hero himself is at one with reality when he goes to meet his doom.

Hegel, above all others, has set forth this interpretation as the one which defines the essential content of tragedy. But in doing this he has so simplified its inner meaning that he is well on the way to depriving it of the genuinely tragic. Indeed, the line that he sees exists, but it is valid only in its indissoluble unity with its opposite — unreconciled self-assertion. Unless understood in this context, Hegel's conception of the tragic ends in trivial harmony and premature contentment.

(c) In witnessing tragedies, we invoke, through tragic knowledge, the Dionysiac feeling of life as understood by Nietzsche. The spectator discovers that doom itself is the triumph of reality, a reality so fundamental that it forever outlives all destruction: in prodigality and in destruction, in danger and in doom, this reality becomes aware of its own supreme power.

(d) According to Aristotle the tragic spectacle brings about catharsis, a purification of the soul. The spectator is filled with pity for the hero and with fear for himself. But in living through these emotions, the spectator is freed from them. He soars because he has been shaken. Emotional freedom flows from passions brought into order.

This much is common to all interpretations: in tragedy we experience fundamental reality made plain, as things break wide open in shipwreck. In tragedy we transcend misery and terror and so move toward essential reality.

4. Deliverance from the Tragic

A poet delivers us from tragedy when he shows us tragedy conquered by the awareness of a larger context of fundamental reality. Either tragedy is merged and reconciled with this reality or else it shrinks before it to mere appearance and proscenium.

5. Greek Tragedy

In the *Eumenides,* Aeschylus portrays the tragic course of events as something belonging to the past. Through the reconciliation of gods and demons with the institution of the Areopagus and the cult of the Eumenides, tragic conflict has given rise to the ordering of human existence in the city-state. The era of tragic heroes is succeeded by the era of law and order, where man lives his life in trusting commitment to his city and its service to the gods. What was tragedy in the dark of night provides the ground for a new life in the light of day.

The *Eumenides* forms the last part of a trilogy, the only complete trilogy preserved for us. All the other surviving Aeschylean dramas are middle parts.[5] Hence they all lack the final solution which probably made up the last part of each trilogy. The *Prometheus,* too, is the center part of a trilogy whose concluding portion probably contained the resolution of divine tragedy into divine order. Aeschylean tragedy is still dominated by Greek piety, here brought to crystalline perfection.

Sophocles, too, is still a believer. His *Oedipus at Colonus* concludes, in a manner comparable to Aeschylus, with a conciliatory act of founding a new institution. There always remains a meaningful relationship between man and god, between human action and divine power. When heroes are doomed incomprehensibly — and this is the theme of tragedy — unaware of guilt, like Antigone, or crushed by guilt, like Oedipus, they submit to the divine will. They accept the reality of the divine, not in knowledge but in trust, and sacrifice to it their own will and existence. Accusation, though for moments it rises irresistibly, at last subsides in lament.

Deliverance from the tragic ends with Euripides. Psychological conflicts, accidents of circumstance, divine intervention (*deus ex machina*), all leave the tragic stripped of context. The individual is thrown back upon his own resources. Despair looms large, together with desperate inquiry into the meaning and goal of life, into the nature of the gods. Not mere lament but accusation now comes to the fore. For brief moments, calm seems to well up from prayer and hearkening to the divine, only to be lost anew in doubt. There is no more deliverance. *Tyche* — chance and fate — takes the place of the gods. Man's limitations and loneliness become frighteningly manifest.

6. *Christian Tragedy*

The believing Christian no longer recognizes tragedy as
genuine. Redemption has occurred and is perpetually
renewed through grace. This untragic approach transforms
man's worldly misery and misfortune into a view of the
world, a view perhaps utterly pessimistic, seeing the world
as but a proving ground where man must earn eternal
salvation. The world exists as a flow of events guided by
Providence. Here all is but way and transition; here nothing is ultimate reality.

To be sure, every form of tragedy is transparent if caught
at the very moment of its transcendence. To be able to
stand fast and to die in the midst of nothingness — this is
"deliverance," but deliverance within the tragic and through
its own efficacy. If there were nothing more than pure
immanence, if we were inescapably confined within the
limits of our existence, then even to stand fast and hold
one's own amidst shipwreck would be meaningless. But
when we thus hold our own we do not overcome immanence by bringing in another world. We do so only by
the very act of transcending, by the knowledge of our
outermost frontiers, and by the insights gained in looking
back from those frontiers. Only a faith that knows another
reality besides immanent reality can bring deliverance from
tragedy. That is the case with Dante, and with Calderón.
With them, knowledge of the tragic, the tragic predica-
ments themselves, and tragic heroism, have all undergone
radical change because these poets have included them

within the plan of Providence and the operation of Grace, a plan and an operation that deliver man from all the vast nothingness and self-destruction in this world.

7. *Philosophic Tragedy*

The philosophic spirit can deliver men from tragedy; but such liberation must extend beyond the tragic. It is not enough that man should endure in silence. And it is not enough that he should merely be ready for the Other, should merely imagine it as a symbol in his daydreams. Rather, tragedy would have to be conquered by turning this Other into a reality, a reality made possible by tragic knowledge but not confined to it. This has been depicted only once in a drama that for this reason is unique — Lessing's *Nathan the Wise,* next to *Faust* the profoundest drama in the German language. But Goethe, although far richer as a poet and much more powerful in his visions, cannot do without the help of Christian symbols; Lessing frugally confines himself to humaneness pure and simple, both undeceiving and undeceived, at the risk of having it mistaken for bareness, for lack of color and of form, unless the reader's own spirit can fill in the clear outlines drawn by the poet.

Lessing wrote this "dramatic poem," as he called it, during the most desperate period of his life, when he was stricken by the death of his wife and son, and embittered by quarrels with the infamous *Hauptpastor* Goetze. To the easy suggestion that in such times of despair one might prefer to forget what the world is really like, Lessing re-

plies: "Not at all: the world as I see it is just as natural;
and it is hardly due to Providence alone that it is not just
as actual in fact." [6] So natural a world, not dominant yet
not unreal, Lessing portrays in his *Nathan.*

Nathan the Wise is not tragedy. When Nathan makes
his appearance at the beginning of the drama, his tragedy
lies in the past. It is behind him, his Job-like fate, the doom
of Assad. The real meaning of the drama first unfolds in
Nathan's person, out of his past tragedy and out of his
present knowledge of the tragic. Tragedy has been conquered — not as in Aeschylus by mythical visualization
of a world guided by Zeus, Dike, and the gods; not as in
Calderón by the certain Christian faith that solves all; not
as in Indian drama by an order of reality taken for granted.
It has been overcome instead by the idea of man's essential
humanity. This idea unfolds as something eternally growing, not as a pattern given once and for all. The idea of
humanity does not reside in the contemplation of a world
perfect and finished. Rather, it dwells in the all-encompassing striving of the men who have this vision: it springs
from their inner activity and finds its fulfillment in their
living communication.

Nathan's soul is both sensitive and sensible. It has found
itself, and it has achieved maturity amid the most terrible
suffering. Thus matured, it seems to reunite mankind as
one great family, long dispersed and unaware of its blood
ties, but now restored to mutual recognition. (In the
drama this is achieved symbolically through an actual
family.) In this Nathan is not guided by any master plan

based on comprehensive knowledge. He works step by step with the aid of whatever knowledge and intimations he derives from any situation, guided by his ever-present love of man. For the ways of man are not rationally purposeful; they are made possible only through strength of heart; and its wisdom is the most prudent of all.

For this reason, the drama shows how everything that was entangled is finally straightened out. Deeds of distrust, suspicion, and enmity are resolved as the inner nature of the persons in the play is revealed. Whatever is done from an impulse of love within the realm of reason is bound to turn out well. Freedom effects freedom. Prudent restraint followed by sudden unmistakable insight, careful planning followed by the breakthrough of unreserved frankness — these mark the meeting of souls which lays the foundation of a solidarity that cannot be shaken. Meanwhile, the base villains who remain outside the family of man are imperceptibly made powerless.

As for the truly human beings, they are not so many identical copies of one single and correct idea of humanity. They are essentially different and unique persons, individualized figures that meet one another, not because they have background or descent in common (for they include as many different types as the Dervish, the Monk, the Knight Templar, Recha, Saladin, and Nathan), but because they follow the same direction toward truth. Each of them gets involved in entanglements peculiar to himself, and by these he is distinguished from the others. All manage to resolve their difficulties: each masters his specific nature

without stifling it. For the lives of all of them are deeply
rooted in common ground: each embodies a particular
form of potential freedom as well as of freedom realized.

In Lessing's drama, reason is tangibly alive in human
personalities. It is the atmosphere of the play — rather
than individual actions and phrases, rather than emotions
and truths — which conveys to us the spirit of the whole.
One must not cling to the subject matter. All that material
is time-bound, not essential: the romantic setting in the
Holy Land at the time of the Crusades, when all peoples and
all men met there and influenced one another; the ideas of
German Enlightenment; the despised Jew as the protagonist
— all these are indispensable visual aids to represent what
no drama in the last analysis can put on the stage. It seems
as if Lessing had tried the impossible and nearly succeeded.
To criticize him for unpoetic abstractions and ideological
bias in favor of the Enlightenment is to cling to mere matters of detail and plot. What seems easiest is actually the
most difficult, not for our eyes or intellect but for our soul.
For we must respond from the depth of our own souls if
we are to feel the enthusiasm of that philosophy, its un-
fathomable sadness, and its smiling calm — if we are to
realize what is essential and unique in Lessing.

Goethe once said that "tragedy disappears to the degree
that an equitable settlement is possible." If we think of
this equitable settlement as a cosmic and transcendent
process, in which everything automatically turns into harmony, we are deceiving ourselves by an illusion — for in
this case the tragic is overlooked, not overcome. By

equitable settlement, however, we can also mean that living communication between human beings which arises in the depth of their struggles from their continuing love for each other, and the mutual bonds which it creates. Far from being an illusion, such solidarity is the existential task of human life. Through it, man overcomes the tragic. Only from this basis can we understand, without self-deception, man's metaphysical conquests over tragedy.

8. *Tragedy Shriveled to Aesthetic Detachment*

Greek tragedy was performed at the feast of Dionysus as a religious ceremony. The medieval mystery play was also tied to religion, in a tradition which later determined Calderón to cast his tragedies in the form of mystery plays. In Shakespeare's England, on the contrary, tragedy marked the achievement of self-knowledge by a vigorous world. At its peak, this tragedy without doubt brought inner liberation, one that provided within this world an experience analogous to a religious rite in lifting up all who took part in it. The great poets were the educators of their people, prophets of their ethos. Their audiences were not only stirred — they were transformed into their real selves.

Always, however, drama and audience degenerate before long into mere functions of a play. The play becomes devoid of moral obligations. Originally, its seriousness had been one way of bringing about "deliverance" by communicating knowledge of the tragic; something happened inside the spectator. But in slowly sinking to the level of a general human craving for passive entertainment, this seriousness evaporated in the pleasant tingle of passive excitement.

It is essential that I not only watch and derive "aesthetic" edification from the tragedy, but also participate in it with my innermost self and act out its insight because of its direct importance to me. The whole content is lost if I think myself safe, or if I look upon the tragic as something alien to myself, or as something that might have involved me but that I have now escaped for good. I would then be looking at the world from the safety of a harbor, as if I were no longer risking body and soul on its troubled seas in search of my destiny. I would see the world in terms of grandiose and tragic interpretations: the world is so made that everything great in it is doomed to perish, and it is so made for the delight of the unconcerned spectator.

To accept this view is to paralyze existential activity. The function of disaster is, then, not to rouse us but to make us accept the world as we find it. And because the world is what it is, I cannot change it and should be glad not to become involved in it myself. But I like to watch disaster from a distance: it is all very well for tragedy to occur at some other place so long as I myself am left in peace. As a spectator I share the sensations, I derive self-satisfaction from the presumed nobility of my emotions, I take sides, pass judgment, allow myself to be shocked — and in reality I stay at a safe distance.

Once before, tragic knowledge was transformed into an affair of aesthetic refinement. That was the case in post-classical antiquity, when the old dramas were revived; and it has happened again in more recent times. Not only the spectator but even the poets themselves lose their former seriousness of purpose. The new nineteenth-century trage-dies were for the most part showpieces of thrilling rhetoric, brilliant and contrived. At one time, deliverance within the tragic had liberated man by letting him see through the tragic, as through a glass, to the unspoken and unutterable depths of life. In the nineteenth century, this deliverance within the tragic is reduced to understanding the philo-sophical theories about the tragic, in their disguise as theatrical figures. Here we have unreality, painted with the resplendent colors of aesthetic staging. There is a dis-crepancy between the artist and his work in this derived culture, and most of his creations lack life and blood. No violence of emotions, no dramatic sequence of events, no skillful handling of scenic efforts can substitute for the infinite depth of Greek tragedy and of Shakespeare. All that remains is thought, sentimentality, and pathos, per-haps even some insights that are valid but unformed. In outstanding poets such as Hebbel and Grillparzer, serious-ness derived from education and culture substitutes for the seriousness of immediate human existence. In the end, their dramatic figures ring hollow to the knock.

CHAPTER FIVE

Fundamental Interpretations of the Tragic

At the edge of doom, the tragic heroes act out the pattern of tragic reality. The poetic work presents this pattern. The heroes put it into words, in general statements about the tragedy of all existence. Knowledge of the tragic becomes itself a basic feature of tragic reality. But the systematic unfolding of a tragic interpretation of the world (a tragic metaphysics) is an intellectual construction that is attempted only in the contemplation of the poetic work, and thus indirectly of reality.

Such reflections of tragic drama upon its own meaning can be systematically arranged and made coherent. Thus they can be made to yield several basic interpretations of tragedy. These can be in terms either of myth or of philosophical concepts. What was earlier said more or less incidentally will now be restated in systematic context.

1. The Mythical Interpretation

Mythical interpretation means thinking in terms of pictures — of pictures taken for realities. Such interpretation dominates Greek tragedy. Tragedy presented with the knowledge of gods and demons as the decisive powers is meaningful only where there is belief in such deities. This puts a certain distance between Greek tragedy and ourselves. We do not sacrifice at the altars of the Greek gods and do not believe in Greek demons. But we can still understand what contents were at work within the forms of ancient tragedy. There is an incomparable fascination in the high seriousness of the thoughts, the questions, and the answers embodied in the concrete images of Greek tragic writings.

By contrast, Shakespeare is close to us because his milieu is close to ours. Thanks to this closeness, Shakespeare can speak on the secular stage and in symbolic ciphers rather than in concrete embodiments of the contents of faith. In Shakespeare we find no Eumenides, no Moira, Apollo, or Zeus, but witches, ghosts, and the magic of fairy tales. There is no Prometheus but a Prospero and an Ariel. No cult serves as framework of the dramatic performance. Instead the poet has the noble task of holding the mirror up to the world, of bearing witness to reality, of making the audience feel the background of meaning, order, law, truth, and divinity. Hence any mythical interpretation of Shakespeare's tragedy is invalid.

Above all, mythical interpretation has reference to the ultimate guidance of things:

Man the planner, arrogating to himself this guidance, must make the experience that — despite his planning — he is still subject to something else, something that is both different and more inclusive. The less he knows, the more sensitive his knowledge of the tragic renders him to all that is still veiled: tragic events are guided by a power that is inexorable.

Within the knowledge of the tragic this guidance is thought of as "destiny." But what is held to be the nature of this destiny will appear in the most different mythical forms. It can be an *impersonal* and *anonymous* curse in consequence of some crime perpetuating itself as family curse, from generation to generation. In Aeschylus and Sophocles its agents are demonic beings such as the Erinyes; the gods know of it beforehand; oracles predict it; and one's own actions can promote or impede it. It is by no means human guilt, always or even most of the time. Rather, the hero is justified in saying:

> I have suffered misery, strangers — suffered it through unwitting deeds, and of those acts — be Heaven my witness! — no part was of mine own choice.
> . . . No wilful sin . . . stainless before the law, void of malice, have I come unto this pass![1]

And summing up:

> . . . how couldst thou justly blame the unknowing deed?[2]

But just as there is curse, there is also *promise*. Promise is as unfailing as curse is pitiless (Oedipus, as promised, finds blessed death in the grove sacred to the Eumenides).

The impersonal and anonymous power is, above all, *Moira,* to whom even gods must submit or with whom, as in Aeschylus, Zeus the supreme god is united.

Tyche, Chance, appearing in Euripides, rules arbitrarily without meaning or reference to the gods. In Hellenistic times, *Tyche* is personified as goddess or demon, and she becomes *Fortuna* to the Romans.

Guidance in Calderón is that *Providence* which as God's inscrutable will leads the soul to its salvation.

Every act of guidance operates through the medium of man's own actions which bring about what man neither contemplates nor desires.

In the mythical view, the world is the arena of forces both divine and demonic. These are interlocked in their anonymous results which appear in persons, actions, and events. If man is to understand all these, he must trace them back to the gods and demons who are their sources.

2. *The Philosophic Interpretations*

Thought seeks to grasp the essential nature of the tragic not in pictures but in concepts. It attempts universal interpretations.

One interpretation locates the tragic in *Being* as such. Whatever exists, exists as self-negation, in the dialectic of Being. Through negation it moves and becomes tragic. God is intrinsically tragic; God suffering the ground of all Being. Such a doctrine of universal tragedy — "pantragism" — is a metaphysic of tragedy as universal phenomenon. The tragedy of this world then follows from a fundamental tragic predicament. Being itself has a crack running through it.

To say that the ground of all Being is tragic, however, seems absurd. Instead of actually transcending our world, this narrow pseudo-insight merely absolutizes one of its aspects. Tragedy resides only in the phenomena of this world. For through the tragic, something different speaks to us, something that is no longer tragic.

Another interpretation locates the tragic in the *world*. In that case, world-wide tragedy is the visible manifestation of universal negativity. This negativity is implicit in the finiteness of all things, in the multiplicity of individual variants, in the struggle of all that exists against all else that exists for self-preservation and supremacy; and this negativity is implicit finally in chance. In this sense the course of this world and the universal destruction of all that has arisen are called tragic.

This view is not content to reduce the tragic to the level of all sorts of evil, misery, and suffering. All of these at least presuppose a living agent to experience them. Actually, this view would stretch the meaning of the tragic to include all negativity in general. Of genuine tragedy, however, one can speak only with reference to man.

Human tragedy can be recognized on two levels:

(a) All human life, activity, achievement, and success are doomed finally to suffer shipwreck. Death, suffering, sickness, and mortality may be veiled from sight, but in the end they engulf all. For life as existence here and now is finite. It is characterized by the multiplicity of elements that mutually exclude and combat one another. Life perishes. To be aware of this is in itself tragic: every particular instance of destruction and every way of suffering that leads to it flow from one basic and all-encompassing reality.

Deeper and truer tragedy arises only where tragic knowledge understands that ruinous conflict is founded in the very nature of truth and goodness, and must inexorably claim its due.

(b) Reality is divided against itself, and so is truth. Truth opposes truth and must defend its own rightful claim not only against injustice, but also against the rightful claims of other truths. Tragedy is real because irreconcilable opposition is real. Mythically, this schism may be reflected in man's obligation to serve many gods, where the service of one impairs or excludes that of another. Or, without such mythical representation, this opposition may be visualized as the battle of every existence against all others. At bottom, all these views agree: human character, mind, and existence are not only linked by common bonds but also forced into combat by their mutual incompatibility. Every moral imperative is tainted by guilt, for it must destroy others equally moral and equally imperative.

Viewed from this perspective, certain distinctions appear which permit us to point out the very essence of the tragic. Without exception, universal shipwreck is the fundamental characteristic of every existence. This includes accidental misfortune, guilt that is specific and avoidable, and the misery of suffering in vain. We find genuine tragedy, how-

ever, only in that destruction which does not prematurely
cut short development and success, but which, instead,
grows out of success itself. Knowledge that life is at the
mercy of blind fate is not yet tragic knowledge. Genuine
tragic knowledge sees deeper. It knows that even in his
last and innermost strongholds of ostensible success and
ostensible security, man is forsaken and abandoned to the
bottomless.

Hence there is no trace of tragic knowledge in the mere
urge to experience shipwreck and suffering. Such knowledge arises only where man actually accepts danger and
that inescapable nexus of guilt and doom implicit in all
true action and accomplishment in the real world.

We will not understand the tragic by thinking in the
alternatives of "success or failure." We can grasp it only
by searching more deeply, by seeing that precisely when
we are most highly successful we most truly fail. Apart
from this there is that failure whose claim to tragedy is
fraudulent, where something merely happened to go wrong,
an accidental mishap, or the perverse striving for failure
instead of for effectiveness, the striving for a disaster that
was not even necessary.

3. Limits of Interpretation

What is consummated under the name of tragic knowledge are the original visions of reality. Compared with
such visions, all interpretations of the tragic are inadequate.
Mythical interpretation itself is just one way of viewing the
tragic, confined to Greek tragedy alone. It would therefore

be absurd to reduce all these visions to a single concept as their common denominator. For as visions they are for- ever either more or less than what concepts can express. To seek specific meanings in single strands of tragic knowl- edge — as in the tragic subjects of literature — is to miss seeing the whole. Interpretations that claim to be the one universal interpretation of the tragic do either of two things: they make it narrow, or else they miss it altogether.

We must therefore distinguish, first, tragic reality as such; second, tragic knowledge as the conscious recognition of this reality; third, the philosophy of the tragic. Tragic reality becomes effective only by means of tragic knowl- edge; this transforms the human personality. The philos- ophy of the tragic, however — its interpretation — goes one of two ways: either it completely perverts tragic knowledge, or it keeps open the wider awareness derived from its own personal and original vision.

4. The Distortion of Tragic Knowledge into a Tragic World View

Every effort to deduce tragedy alone as the dominant law of reality is philosophically unsound. We object to it, as to every metaphysics that would approach Being and Reality deductively and that would make descriptive state- ments about the nature of Being or God — we object to it because it seeks to make them both absolute and finite. Even those profound dualisms which are postulated as existing at the very base of reality and assumed to account for the origin of tragedy (for instance, that aspect of God

which is not Himself) are only code symbols of relative
validity within philosophic thought, and no deductive
knowledge can be derived from them. Tragic knowledge is
open knowledge, well aware of its own ignorance. To
freeze it into a pan-tragism of whatever kind is to distort it.

How a tragic philosophy becomes narrow and perverted
may be studied in the case of the poet Hebbel. His systematic interpretation becomes absurd, monstrous, and
fanatical. The result is poetry contrived by speculation,
the loss of all true spiritual depth — poetry reduced on the
one hand to nothing but psychology, and on the other to
speculatively heightened grandeur. At the same time, as in
flashes of lightning, Hebbel achieves some striking insights
and perspectives. But his consciousness of tragedy is no
more than consciousness of misery decked out in philosophic trimmings.

As a concept of aesthetics, too, the tragic has acquired
a coloring which corresponds to this misleading type of
tragic philosophy, as when Bahnsen speaks of tragedy as
the universal law, or Unamuno of the tragic sense of life.

The most sublime aberration of a tragic world view occurs when the truly tragic is turned into an absolute and
made to appear as if it constituted the essence and value
of man.

Tragedy is distinct from misfortune, suffering, and destruction, from sickness or death, and from evil. It is so
distinct by virtue of the nature of its knowledge; this knowledge is general, not special; it is question, not acceptance
— accusation, not lament. Tragic knowledge is further

distinct by virtue of the close connection between truth and catastrophe: tragedy grows more intense as the clashing forces increase in scale and as the necessity of their conflict deepens. All misfortune becomes tragic only through the context in which it occurs, or to which we relate it; through the consciousness and knowledge of those who suffer and those who love; through the interpretation, by tragic knowledge, of misfortune as meaningful. But in and for itself, misfortune is not tragic; it is simply the burden that all must bear. Tragic knowledge invades and breaks through, but does not master, reality — there is too much it leaves untouched, forgotten, or unexplained. It lures us into an exalting realm of grandeur; and thus, despite all clear-eyed honesty, it obscures the truth.

Tragedy becomes the privilege of the exalted few — all others must be content to be wiped out indifferently in disaster. Tragedy then becomes a characteristic not of man, but of a human aristocracy. As the code of privilege, this philosophy becomes arrogant and unloving; it gives us comfort by pandering to our self-esteem.

Tragic knowledge thus has its limits: it achieves no comprehensive interpretation of the world. It fails to master universal suffering; it fails to grasp the whole terror and insolubility in men's existence. This is clearly shown by the fact that although everyday realities — such as sickness, death, chance, misery, and malice — may well become the media through which tragedy makes its appearance, they are not so considered from the outset simply because they are not in themselves tragic. A tragic philosophy lives in

an aura of grandeur; it offers us personal fulfillment, as
the fortunate result of an appropriately successful disaster,
and thus lifts us high above reality. But in so doing, this
philosophy narrows down our awareness. For in so far as
men find release in an experience of this kind, they find it
only at the price of concealing from themselves the terrifying abysses of reality. Misery — hopeless, meaningless,
heart-rending, destitute, and helpless misery — cries out
for help. But the reality of all this misery without greatness
is pushed aside as unworthy of notice by minds that are
blind with exaltation. And all the while, man presses for
redemption from his terrible realities, which lack the
glamor of tragedy.

Together with this unloving blindness, we find a watered-
down aesthetic jargon in current phrases about tragedy, a
jargon that conveys the essence of tragedy but at the same
time distorts its meaning. This jargon untruthfully makes
reality appear remote, and all too easily relieves us from
having to see the misery of the world as it really is. Thus
it is glibly remarked that tragedy reveals the worthlessness
of life itself, of all individual finite human life; that the
doom of greatness is precisely one of its characteristics;
that the world is set up to break and destroy the unusual
individual. By such diffuse generalities, so plausible in
their vagueness, we cover up the actual ills of reality with
a tissue of lies.

In all tragic philosophies the polarity of tragic knowledge
has been lost. In the original vision, tragedy and the release from it are linked together. But if we rob tragedy of

its opposite pole and isolate it as nothing-but-tragedy, we fall into a bottomless chasm where none of the great tragic compositions have been built.

Wherever total lack of faith seeks to parade as form, it finds the philosophy of nothing-but-tragedy well suited as a camouflage for nothingness. Tragic grandeur is the prop whereby the arrogant nihilist can elevate himself to the pathos of feeling himself a hero. Where seriousness has been lost, an experience of pseudo-seriousness is produced by the violent stimulant of tragedy. The racial past, the sagas, and Greek tragedy are all invoked. Yet what had then been the reality of faith becomes now a deliberate and dishonest substitute for nothingness. The old beliefs are used as phrases to lend a heroic cast to the very un-heroic degeneration of one's own existence, or else to lend a cheap aura of heroism to a life lived in comfort and security.

Such perversion of tragic philosophy then sets free the turmoil of dark impulses: the delight in meaningless ac-tivity, in torturing and in being tortured, in destruction for its own sake, in the raging hatred against the world and man coupled with the raging hatred against one's own despised existence.

CHAPTER SIX

The Insufficiency of
Tragic Knowledge

Instead of systematizing tragic knowledge through speculative deduction, instead of stripping it of its polarity and turning it into a philosophic absolute, we must instead so understand tragic knowledge as to preserve it as an original experience. The original tragic vision consists in thoughts and questions experienced in concrete images. What is more, this form of tragic knowledge always contains the final release from tragedy, not through doctrine and revelation but through the vision of order, justice, love of one's fellow man; through trust; through an open mind and the acceptance of the question as such, unanswered.

Tragic knowledge mounts in intensity through contradictions which it leaves unresolved but which it does not freeze as necessarily insoluble. Hence, tragic knowledge is all imperfection; and perfection is found only in experience as such, in the movement of asking question after question.

We must preserve this original vision of tragic experience. We must keep unobstructed our view of the essential historical context within which the vision of the tragic first arises and in which it finds fulfillment. We must not clamor for explanations of whatever has been, will be, and always is, but we must listen for that which is trying to speak to us. It is not the task of philosophy to transfer by analogy tragic categories from a limited knowledge of the world to a comprehensive knowledge of all reality, but rather to discover a language in the code-symbols we hear. This is why myths, images, and stories of tragic inspiration are quite capable of containing truth without losing their uncommitted, hovering character.

If preserved in its purity, the original vision of the tragic already contains the essence of philosophy: movement, question, open-mindedness, emotion, wonder, truthfulness, lack of illusion.

Philosophy refers to tragic knowledge as to what is inexhaustible in original vision and experience. Philosophy can feel the identity of its own content with the tragic vision of, say, Shakespeare, without being able to put it into identical words. But philosophy refuses to cast this control into the fixed rational terms of a "tragic philosophy of life."

The account we have given of the manifold aspects of the Encompassing, the multiplicity of its divisions, and the idea of its unity — all this defines the framework within which tragic knowledge must be interpreted. Tragedy arises wherever in the world there is disunity, and where its consequences become visible. To be able to say this requires no deduction, but simply an elucidation of what is before us. This failure to achieve unity underlies the ruin of all we see around us. Because unity fails in our temporal existence, it appears to us in the guise of the tragic.

This is, however, tantamount to saying that tragedy is not absolute but belongs in the foreground. Tragedy belongs neither in the realm of transcendence nor in the Basis of all Being, but in the world of sense and time.

1. Truth Rooted and Achieved in the Philosophic Process

We saw that tragic knowledge confronted man's search for truth with an alternative: either to live and err, or to grasp truth and die of it. But it was only a later rational interpretation, not the openness of tragic knowledge itself, that blundered into this rigid either-or. Against the lurid grandeur of this choice we must set this: truth, whole and complete — whether as the source of death or of peace — is not available to us in life and time. Within time, truth is forever under way, always in motion and not final even in its most marvelous crystallizations. Never to retreat from this fundamental situation — that is the condition on which alone philosophic thought can remain truthful.

Tragic knowledge, in its open-mindedness, has not yet abandoned this path. Rather, to take a relative truth for absolute is itself a tragic perversion, a fit object for tragic knowledge. Every truth that we may think complete will prove itself untruth at the moment of shipwreck.

2. The Way and the Movement

Since there is no complete truth, our movement toward it is itself the only form in which truth can achieve completion in existence, here and now. In its very process the boundless acquisition of truth experiences that completion which it never reaches as a goal. The single idea that has been guiding us through the whole of philosophical logic has been the idea of the thinker unswerving on his way.

He is aware of what he knows and what he does not know. He does not fall prey to the falsehood of a truth completed and whole. He lives the meaning of truth in all the ways of being truthful. He is involved in ever deepening communication.

This is the vision of a great and noble life: to endure ambiguity in the movement of truth and to make light shine through it; to stand fast in uncertainty; to prove capable of unlimited love and hope.

Sources of Jaspers' Style

The Introduction, Postscript, and Notes of this book are progressively more detailed attempts to re-create for the reader some of the thousand-page context from which our section on tragedy is taken. In the Introduction, the editor has outlined the general background of Jaspers' philosophy. In the Postscript, some difficulties encountered in attempting to translate Jaspers are shown to stem directly from stylistic qualities — freshness, sweep, and metaphorical compression — rooted in the very fiber of his thought. In the Notes, we cite the original German expression whenever a question as to precise meaning arises.

It is always difficult to define the relationship between the thought and expression of a particular work, because to attempt to infer one from the other involves us in circular reasoning. We need some fixed points on which to hinge our argument.

In the case of Jaspers, there are two distinct sources from which we can obtain help. There are, first, the points his language shares with that of related thinkers. Then, there is the important section of *Von der Wahrheit* (pages

395-449) where he explicitly discusses the place of language in philosophy. We shall take up each in turn.

A great variety of works of different periods, genres, and languages has been labeled "existentialist." Even granting all individual differences, the most casual reader is bound to be struck by two common qualities: marked novelty of approach coupled with marked novelty of expression.

New is the shift of our attention from the study of abstract essences to human existence. This shift, we find, has made language itself problematical. We feel that what these authors are trying to communicate either borders on the ineffable or else can be expressed only in a radically revised version of our inherited language.

Now, many others beside the "existentialists" proper, writers and poets as well as philosophers, have had to face this central problem of communication. As in physics the "field"-concept has given rise to a whole new vocabulary, so in literature the growing view of human reality as nothing but a variable function of innumerable personal perspectives has given rise to the "stream of consciousness" technique. In poetry, adjectives once the ornaments of static substance in human perspective have come to absorb the function of adverbs and refract a whole universe of nothing but perspectives. Nouns and verbs have seen their traditional contrasts merged in a system of pure relation, as nominalized verbs have progressively taken the place of static nouns. Philosophers, always vitally concerned with communication, range all the way from radical to conservative in their attitude toward conventional language. Most today would accept Kant's "Copernican" act of subordinating metaphysical "truth" to "meaning." They differ on its implications — unseen by Kant — for "the intra-subjective *a priori* of language" (Herder).

By declaring truth or falsity meaningless beyond what is "operationally" verifiable, many physicists and logicians make Kant's reduction a total one. They use conventional language only to describe physical or logical operations. Otherwise, they employ specially devised symbolic codes, similar to those used in algebra and chemistry. Others (e.g., Cassirer, and, recently, Mrs. Langer) prefer to include in their concept of "meaning" not only physical or logical operations but all forms of what they take to be man's most basic operation: the symbolic transformation of *all* experience, as documented by anthropology and cultural history. The difference between natural and "human" sciences shrinks to one of degree. Conventional language is revalidated, though only as the readiest among many possible symbolic forms of expression, from religious ritual to algebraic symbols.

The existentialists have not gone this far. Out of concern for human existence as the source of all meaning, they have had to accept cultural history with all its symbolic import. Yet, impressed by man's failures and limits, they have felt that the history of his cultural achievements is only one aspect of his true existence. This is why they have not followed the logicians' example and adopted the minimal language of signs and operational definitions. The very illogicalities of language are seen as failure and limit, as clues to man's true nature. Opinions diverge as to the location and availability of this human nature. Some, like Heidegger, would harness etymology to the task of tracing back through history the symbolism that is metaphor in language in order to recover literal root-meanings. These are to enable the modern philosopher to recapture a pre-historical, pre-symbolic level of human experience and to rebuild philosophy afresh in terms of it.

To Jaspers, this is an illusory search. The only way to man's nature leads through the symbolism by which it functions as historical existence — specifically through the symbolism of all language, metaphor. For there are no literal root-meanings: all words are metaphors more or less faded. Jaspers would redirect our attention to the two characteristics of metaphor. These are ambiguity and transparency on the one hand, and the perpetual motion of self-transcendence on the other. Thus metaphor simultaneously mirrors an infinite number of other metaphors and points beyond itself, beyond language and thought to the things "in themselves." These it reflects without embodying them. As the ambiguity of all consciousness, metaphor reduces the difference between concept and raw experience to one of degree. Still, though self-transcendent, metaphor forever fails to make us conscious of more than the existence of a reality behind the appearances. And even this it does only negatively, by its very failure.

Metaphor, then, as the spectrum of all consciousness, explains the irruption of poetry, art, and religion into

Jaspers' philosophical horizon — over and above logic and etymology. Man's common experience of failure is differently expressed in each and thereby confirmed as real. Jaspers scans all forms, including tragedy as the poetic one, for clues to our own predicament.

The universality of metaphor precludes fixing on any one meaning as the "real" one. Still, we need not engage in the futility of infinite regress. Nor can we, with the logicians, escape into a set of clearly defined symbols to avoid the difficulties of an existence experienced as metaphorical. Instead, to be truly logical we must capture the logic and language of that existence itself, not of some special convention. Here also lies the explanation of Jaspers' sub-title — "Philosophical Logic" — for his major work *On Truth*.

To the extent, therefore, that a philosopher reduces his words to signs and devises a verbal algebra of terms with fixed meanings, he betrays the very movement that is philosophy. Similarly, the superstition that to express all is to know and control all produces only formulas of illusory value. The slogans of "group think" and social engineering are random examples of such reductive fallacy.

To use language is to create new usages. To formulate an idea is to experience that idea. To repeat an idea, one's own or somebody else's, is to re-create for oneself the experience which accompanied its birth. A philosopher, therefore, cannot afford the risk and the temptation of terminology or even of an aesthetic concern with words. They hide from him the limits of his knowledge where failure becomes the source of deeper insight and renewed effort. Language is at its strongest, truest, and least deceptive only where it is the almost unconscious by-product of thinking.

Thus far Jaspers. It is easy to see that he has here uncovered the roots of his own style: his avoidance of terminology, formulas, jargon, his language of metaphor to convey the universality and failure of metaphor. He well realizes that this increase in truthfulness is one of difficulty also and does not make for increased popularity. We prefer to repeat neat formulas to being personally involved in the philosophic process. Still, he asks us to look upon metaphor in philosophy as a challenge, not a drawback, to look in it for what is not only picturesque but true. Thus, in largely substituting nominalized verbs for the traditional "substantive," Jaspers — like the more extreme existentialists — has accommodated the modern sense of universal movement, perspectivism, interrelation. But by doing this as an act of conscious metaphor, he retains, unlike them, the certainty and dignity of Being, however reflected. No doubt the well-known scope in German for such new formations has been a contributing factor. This has, as a matter of historical fact, enabled many German philosophers to do more than translate, to rethink in amazingly similar terms a good deal of pre-Socratic philosophy.

But, forewarned by Jaspers, we must beware of inferring automatic identity of meaning where there is identity of words. Thus, the Encompassing — once believed to be an Aristotelian coinage — has now been shown (W. Jaeger) to go back to Anaximander himself, who applied it to his Infinite as an attribute of the divine. It is tempting but extremely dangerous to use this evidence for inferences about Jaspers' Encompassing.

In conclusion, it may be noted how Jaspers' abstract and dramatic style is sometimes most naturally rendered by terms taken from Shakespeare, from the King James Version of the Bible, or from the English speech of our own day.

HARALD A. T. REICHE

Bibliography

For the sake of convenience, Jaspers' work may be grouped under three headings:

I. His work in psychology

1. *Allgemeine Psychopathologie.* Berlin: Springer. (1st ed., 1913; 5th ed., 1946.) 748 pages.
2. *Psychologie der Weltanschauungen.* Berlin: Springer. (1st ed., 1919; 3rd ed., 1925.) 486 pages.

II. His major philosophical works

1. *Philosophie.* 3 volumes. Berlin: Springer. (1st ed., 1932; 2nd ed., 1948.) 913 pages.
2. *Nietzsche, Einführung, etc.* Berlin: de Gruyter. (1st ed., 1936; 3rd ed., 1949.) 487 pages.
3. *Von der Wahrheit.* Vol. I of *Philosophische Logik.* Munich: Piper. (1947.) 1126 pages.

III. His lesser works

1. *Descartes und die Philosophie.* Berlin: de Gruyter. (1st ed., 1937; 2nd ed., 1948.) 104 pages.
2. *Der philosophische Glaube.* Munich: Piper. (1st ed., 1948; 3rd ed., 1951.) 156 pages.
3. *Die geistige Situation der Zeit.* Berlin: de Gruyter. (1st ed., 1931; 7th ed., 1949.) 191 pages.
4. *Die Idee der Universität.* Berlin: Springer. (1946.) 132 pages.
5. *Die Schuldfrage.* Heidelberg: Schneider. (1946.) 96 pages.
6. *Vom Ursprung und Ziel der Geschichte.* Zurich: Artemis. (1949.) 349 pages.
7. *Einführung in die Philosophie.* (12 radio talks.) Zurich: Artemis. (1st ed., 1949; 2nd ed., 1950.)
8. *Rechenschaft und Ausblick.* (Collection of 21 essays and addresses.) Munich: Piper. (1951.) 368 pages.

Up to the present, only four of these are available — in whole or in part — in English translation:

> *Man in the Modern Age.* Translation by E. Paul of *Die geistige Situation der Zeit* (III-3 on list above). London: George Routledge & Sons, 1933.

> *The European Spirit.* Translation by R. Smith of an essay in *Rechenschaft und Ausblick* (III-8 on list above). London: Student Christian Movement Press, 1948.

> *The Perennial Scope of Philosophy.* Translation by R. Manheim of *Der philosophische Glaube* (III-2 on list above). New York: Philosophical Library, 1949.

> *Way to Wisdom.* Translation by R. Manheim of *Einführung in die Philosophie* (III-7 on list above). New Haven: Yale University Press, 1951.

It is important to note that none of these translations has ventured beyond the more essayistic items of Group III into Group II — which constitutes the massive core of Jaspers' work.

At least until *Von der Wahrheit* is entirely available in English, it would be unfair to send the reader unfamiliar with German to the English translations of Jaspers. Few thinkers have so consistently stressed the importance of acquiring the "long breath" of sustained philosophical effort, as we meet it in Plato, Kant, and Jaspers' own major work.

In the meantime, the reader may be referred to some of the more valuable surveys. Outstanding among these is:

> James Collins. *The Existentialists.* Chicago: Henry Regnery Company, 1952.

Collins devotes thirty-four pages to a critical study of Jaspers, and ten pages to a fine selected bibliography on the philosopher. For an equally brilliant introduction to existentialism (rather than to individual existentialists), see:

> Helmut Kuhn. *Encounter with Nothingness.* Hinsdale, Ill.: Henry Regnery Company, 1949.

For a lucid and profusely documented account of individual topics as historical background to Jaspers' thought, see:

Erich Frank. *Philosophical Understanding and Religious Truth*. New York: Oxford University Press, 1945.

As for recommended reading on the subject of tragedy, there are — in addition to the primary sources used by Jaspers himself — two works of Jaspers' one-time Heidelberg colleague, the sociologist and historian Alfred Weber (brother of the late Max Weber):

A. Weber. *Kulturgeschichte als Kultursoziologie*. Munich: Piper. (1st ed., 1935; 2nd ed., 1950.)

Here Weber, on the sociological and historical level, independently (see page 410, note 1), extends and confirms Jaspers. But even more important is the following:

A. Weber. *Das Tragische und die Geschichte*. Hamburg: Goverts, 1943. 447 pages.

In this book, Weber traces the structure of tragedy from its earliest manifestations through its Greek climax. In many ways, the evidence here presented it closely related to Jaspers' point of view on tragedy and makes ideal collateral reading.

Finally, the Jaspers volume projected by Paul A. Schilpp for his "Library of Living Philosophers" series (Evanston, Ill.) should prove helpful.

Notes

Short titles used in this section refer to books discussed in the Bibliography (pages 113-15).

1. Yet, if spirituality and inwardness are taken (with John H. Finley, Jr.) as the *Iliad's* tragic qualities, then surely the *Odyssey* with its intellectuality and social ethos is far closer to high comedy.

1a. *Weisen des Scheitern*: lit., "ways of stranding or of suffering shipwreck." This is Jaspers' term for failure. Though a language of seafarers, English does not use "shipwreck" in this sense. Much could be made of the apparent paucity in modern English and American of a vocabulary for failure as opposed to one for success; failure tends to be seen solely as an unfortunate interlude, briefly acknowledged but passed over as without positive significance. By contrast, German thought, quite apart from the Existentialist movement, is "conditioned" by its very language and literary tradition to dwell on failure as a general process with a discernible structure. For various kinds of failure — linguistic, tragic, philosophical — see the Postscript; and compare, below, Note 2 of Chapter IV.

2. *Theogony,* lines 98-103. Jack Lindsay translation in *The Oxford Book of Greek Verse in Translation* (New York: Oxford University Press, 1938), p. 149. Reprinted by permission of the Clarendon Press, Oxford.

3. *Das Selbstsein des Menschen*: lit., "selfhood." By "selfhood" Jaspers means individual consciousness and conscious inner activity — the process as its own product. Man is aware of his own inner tensions and his inner activity in shaping them and making them conscious. See *Von der Wahrheit,* pp. 540 ff.

4. *Seinsvergewisserung.* This involves verifying one's own inner condition and relationship with one's environment.

5. *Nichtwissen.* This is not so much "ignorance" as "inability to know more"; the negation refers to the future rather than to the present.

6. This, of course, merely completes a process begun as early as Hesiod and Xenophanes. See Werner Jaeger, *The Theology of the Early Greek Philosophers* (New York: Oxford University Press, 1948); and F. Solmsen, *Hesiod and Aeschylus* (Ithaca: Cornell University Press, 1949).

7. *Selbstsein.*

8. *Das Zerrissene.* Kuhn, *Encounter*, pp. 124 ff., shows how this term was first used in the early Hegel's theological writing to denote — in Kantian terms — the critical mental "cleavage" suffered by the Jews previous to the coming of Christ.

9. *Durch die offene Bruchfläche.*

CHAPTER II

Basic Characteristics of the Tragic

1. *Dasein* is man's empirical, worldly existence. It is sharply distinguished from the authentic existence that is the Uncharted Background. But for the sake of readability, *Dasein* has often been rendered simply as "existence." Where Jaspers' context has left some doubt as to which is meant (as in Note 8 of Chapter II), the German has been given in the note.

2. *Menschsein.*

3. *Tragische Haltung.* This is the inner attitude of composure in the face of tragedy; it resembles Hamlet's "the readiness is all."

4. *Im Akt seines Selbstseins.* The inner movement implied in Note 3 of Chapter I is here explicitly stated: selfhood is the product and the activity of consciousness.

5. *Weltsein.* As the sum of all knowable objects in our experience, this includes ourselves as part of this world. See *Von der Wahrheit*, pp. 88 ff.

5a. Editor's version of Jaspers' excerpt from Kshemisvara, *Kausikas Zorn,* as edited and translated into German by L. Fritze

(Leipzig: Reclam, 1882), p. 64. Innocent King Haristshandra is cruelly destroyed by the magician Kausika. For a detailed discussion of the sense in which this, and Indic drama generally is "tragic," see Weber, *Das Tragische,* pp. 125-78.

6. *Weltstimmung.*

7. *Betroffenheit.* In English, to be "perplexed" is to be baffled by circumstance. In German, however, one is *betroffen* when one is not only baffled but touched to one's core.

8. *Schuld des Daseins schlechthin*: lit., "the guilt of human existence as such."

9. This was the "Orphic" view of Rohde and Nietzsche, now generally abandoned on the basis of new manuscript evidence brought forward by Diels. See, e.g., Jaeger, *Theology,* pp. 34 ff.

10. *Schuld des Soseins.* This is guilt, not of existence, origin, or action, but arising from the stubbornness and meanness in one's character.

11. *Im Bösen sich vernichtigend.* This implies both physical and spiritual self-destruction.

12. Plato, *Republic,* VI, 491 e, 495 b. Shorey translation (Loeb Classical Library).

CHAPTER III

THE PROBLEM OF TRUTH

1. *Oedipus at Colonus,* lines 963-64 and 966-68. In this as in all other translations from the Greek, the aim has been to preserve the connotation emphasized by Jaspers. This aim has been fulfilled either by selecting from a variety of available English translations, or else, as here, by doing Jaspers into English directly controlled only by the Greek.

2. *Oedipus Tyrannus.* Lines 316-17: R. C. Jebb translation (Cambridge, England, 1887). Lines 328-29: Dudley Fitts and Robert Fitzgerald translation (New York: Harcourt, Brace, 1949), pp. 23-24.

3. Line 398. E. F. Watling translation in *The Theban Plays* (Harmondsworth, Middlesex, England: Penguin Classics, 1949), p. 37.

4. Line 412. Watling translation, p. 37.

5. Lines 828-29. Jebb translation.

6. Lines 832-33. David Grene translation in *Three Greek Plays in Translation* (Chicago: University of Chicago Press, 1942), p. 123. Reprinted by permission of the University of Chicago Press.

7. Lines 977-83, 1061. Grene translation.

8. Line 1065, Watling translation, p. 55.

9. Line 1272. Jebb translation.

10. Lines 1186-95. Jebb translation.

11. Line 1347. For version, see Note 1 to Chapter III.

12. For much in the following interpretations I am indebted to Karl Werder, *Vorlesungen über Shakespeares Hamlet* (Berlin: 1st ed., 1859-60; 2nd ed., 1893). [*Jaspers' Note.*]

13. I, v, 189-90.

14. II, ii, 178-79.

15. I, v, 128-32.

16. II, ii, 593-95.

17. III, i, 83-88.

18. IV, iv, 32-33, 40-46.

19. I, iv, 65.

20. I, iv, 82-84.

21. V, ii, 355-60.

22. III, ii, 68-79.

23. V, ii, 399-401.

24. V, ii, 408-09.

25. V, ii, 367.

26. IV, iv, 53-56, 59-62.

27. II, ii, 116-19.

28. V, ii, 230-35.

29. V, ii, 7-11.

30. I, v, 166-67.

31. I, v, 21-22.

32. V, ii, 369.

33. V, ii, 370-71.

CHAPTER IV

THE SUBJECTIVITY OF THE TRAGIC

1. Jaspers' word *Erlösung* covers the meaning of both "deliverance" (which does not require sacrifice) and "redemption" (which does). These terms have been used interchangeably here as the context seemed to require.

2. *Grenzsituation*: lit., "limit-situation." There is really no English phrase of comparable generality that can mean both "limit" and "limit of our powers." It is characteristic of Jaspers, the psychologist and philosopher, that he has succeeded in endowing Kant's sober "marginal concept" with all the pathos of human existence. On failure, see Note 1a of Chapter I.

3. *Aufgehoben* — lit., "lifted up and preserved" — is the technical term introduced by Hegel to describe the manner in which contraries are eliminated, yet preserved in synthesis on a higher plane.

4. *Aufgehoben.*

5. Aeschylus' *Persians*, though, is now generally thought to be second in an unconnected trilogy, and *Prometheus Bound* first in a *Prometheia* trilogy.

6. *Works*, edited by Lachmann and Muncker (Leipzig: Göschen, 1897), Vol. XIII, p. 337.

CHAPTER V

FUNDAMENTAL INTERPRETATIONS OF THE TRAGIC

1. *Oedipus at Colonus*, lines 521-23, 529, 548. R. C. Jebb translation.

2. Line 977. Jebb translation.

Index